Expository Preaching

Expository Preaching

Principles and practice

Haddon W. Robinson

Foreword by J. A. Motyer

INTER-VARSITY PRESS

Inter-Varsity Press
38 De Montfort Street, Leicester LE1 7GP

© 1980 by Baker Book House Company, USA

First British edition 1986
Reprinted 1989, 1991, 1992, 1994, 1997

British Library Cataloguing in Publication Data

Robinson, Haddon W.
  [Biblical preaching] Expository
  preaching: its principles and practice.
  1. Bible—Homiletical use
  2. Preaching
  I. [Biblical preaching]   II. Title
  251   BV4211.2

ISBN 0-85110-758-3

Typeset in the United States of America
Printed in Great Britain by Galliard (Printers) Ltd, Great Yarmouth

*Inter-Varsity Press is the book-publishing division of the Universities
and Colleges Christian Fellowship (formerly the Inter-Varsity
Fellowship), a student movement linking Christian Unions in
universities and colleges throughout the United Kingdom and the
Republic of Ireland, and a member movement of the International
Fellowship of Evangelical Students. For information about local
and national activities write to UCCF, 38 De Montfort Street,
Leicester LE1 7GP.*

To the men and women
who keep a sacred appointment
on Sunday morning.
Bewildered by seductive voices,
nursing wounds life has inflicted upon them,
anxious about matters that do not matter.
Yet they come to listen for a clear word from God
that speaks to their condition.

And to those who minister to them now
and those who will do so in the future.

Contents

Foreword

The preacher and preaching in the plan of God

In every church and fellowship, no matter how small, even how run down, Sunday offers the biggest and most important opportunity for teaching the faith and sharing in the truth. But many ministers are only too aware that their performance as preachers falls short of what they would wish. It is good to reach out to such with a word of encouragement and to commend to them a book so full of practical help and counsel. In many circles, however, the appearance of such a book is more likely to provoke a yawn. For there are those who have come to regard preaching as outmoded and irrelevant, superseded by other means of communicating the gospel such as dialogue, discussion and drama.

In this climate of opinion the *case* for preaching has to be made out if there is to be a renewal of confidence in preaching. This we shall attempt to do in the conviction that the greatest need in the church today, in both pulpit and pew, is a recovery of the biblical view of preaching.

No-one who wishes to think biblically about the work of the preacher could start at a better point than Acts 15:7. It gives us much more than a launching pad: for, to be exact, it is a prism which radiates the primary colours of the Bible's spectrum of preaching.

The shape of the verse

If we set the verse out as a diagram, its meaning at once becomes plain:

> GOD made CHOICE that → through my MOUTH
> the Gentiles should HEAR
> the word of the gospel
> and BELIEVE

Obviously a verse like this is definitive about the place and essential nature of preaching: it is God's chosen procedure for bringing his truth to the world. But equally it takes the preacher beyond (if we may, for a moment, so speak) the bare duty of preaching as an act of obedience to the divine will. It lifts and encourages us by insisting that the same sovereign choice determines that preaching will be fruitful. For, taking the elements of God's choice in order, he chooses the preacher ('through my mouth'), the audience and the message ('the Gentiles ... the word of the gospel') – and he chooses the outcome, that they should respond in faith and 'believe'. The gracious will of God embraces both that the preacher should work and there should be fruit as a result.

God's purpose

The Lord is not above using a pun to make his point. He called Jeremiah's attention to an almond bud (Heb. *šāqēḏ*) in order to say to his timid messenger, 'I am watching over (*šōqēḏ*) my word to perform it' (Je. 1:11–12). There we have in (almost literally) a nutshell what the Bible returns to again and again. Just as behind the tender almond blossom there is the surging power of God, breaking winter's grip, bringing life, warmth and beauty, so behind the unimpressiveness of the thing preached (1 Cor. 1:21) and the weakness of the preacher (1 Cor. 2:3–4) God's mighty Spirit is about his work.

The single-mindedness of the Lord in this matter ought not to be overlooked. Jeremiah may have been one of the many who find it difficult to leave bed in the mornings: at any rate, he found no better metaphor for the divine urgency over preaching than to say that the Lord 'rose early' to send prophets to his people[1] – men of the word, preachers. The heart of their calling was to say, on the basis of their unique inspiration, 'This is what the Lord says'. And when, through the ministry of the Lord Jesus, the prophetic order was replaced by the apostolic order and the apostolic church, the same divine desire and urgency was given effect in a command to preach everywhere,[2] to see the preaching ministry as the irreplaceable essential[3] and a thing which God himself and the returning Lord Jesus would bring under scrutiny and judgment.[4] At the summit of Old Testament Messianism stands a preaching Servant: his calling is to bring forth God's revealed truth to the whole world[5] and to this end God has made his mouth like a sharp sword, pointed, effective,[6] yet also gentle and seasonable to the weary.[7] He is to be, himself, God's salvation to the ends of the earth.[8] As such, he fulfils, on the one hand, what Moses, his greatest and normative predecessor as prophet, had forecast;[9] on the other hand, his own prophetic ministry finds its completion in the work of the preachers whom he sends out, through whose word 'as many as were ordained to eternal life believed'.[10] Pictorially – but much more than

---

1. *E.g.* Je. 7:25; 25:4; 26:5; 29:19; *etc.*   2. *E.g.* Mt. 28:18–20; Acts 1:8.
3. *E.g.* Acts 6:2,4; 1 Cor. 1:17; 9:16.   4. 2 Tim. 4:1.   5. Is. 42:1, 3–4.
6. Is. 49:2.   7. Is. 50:4.   8. Is. 49:6.   9. Dt. 34:10.
10. Acts 13:46–49.

a mere picture, a fact and a dynamic reality – Revelation 10:1–11 catches the spirit of the whole Bible and the mind of God in Christ: the Lord Jesus stands with mighty authority upon land and sea alike and the voice which expresses his authority finds its message in the unimpressiveness of a little book, opened in his hand (v.2). The book is given to his prophetic minister (vv.8–11) as the substance of world-wide preaching. Thus, when the weak, human voice of preaching gives expression to the message of the opened book, the actual speaker is he whose voice is as a lion and who commands all the forces of creation (vv.3–4).

The preacher and the book

The Lord graciously calls his servants to a prophetic ministry, as this passage in Revelation shows[11] and therefore, like all prophetic ministry, our preoccupation is with the Word of God. Yet our ministry is not identical with theirs whom Jesus called 'your predecessors, the prophets'[12] for, in human terms, their ministry originated the Word of God, whereas ours derives from it. Putting the matter bluntly, they wrote the Bible; we preach it. We have the authority of the risen Lord for seeing things like this. Like all the Gospel writers, Luke begins his revelation of the risen Lord with the discovery of the empty tomb (Lk. 24:1–12). Following this, like Matthew and John, he proceeds to portray what sort of person the risen Lord showed himself to be, and his resurrection narrative comes as the natural climax of his Gospel. Refusing to allow the Emmaus walkers in the first instance to have a direct knowledge of himself (24:16), he undertakes (as they later described it) to 'open the scriptures' (vv.27,32). When they had carried their testimony to the risen Lord back to Jerusalem, Jesus himself came to the larger company and

---

11. Rev. 10:7,11; see esp. Acts 2, where the pentecostal gift (vv.2–4) enabled the preaching of an intelligible word (vv.4,6,8) and fulfilled the prediction of the raising up of prophets (vv.17–18).   12. Mt. 5:12.

'opened their minds to understand the scriptures' (v.45), telling them that 'thus it is written' so that thus it might be preached (vv.46–47). The intention of Luke regarding the risen Lord is thus plain: Jesus insists that he must be first known through the Scriptures and then, through the same Scriptures, shared with the world: he opens the Scriptures to his preachers – and opens their minds to understand – so that they may share the opened book with others.

At the other end of the apostolic period Paul had the same vision and concern. As he wrote his second letter to Timothy he was aware of his own impending death (4:6–8). This single fact makes the letter of crucial interest for us for, while Paul looked forward to his death, we look back to the end of the apostolic age and the beginning of the post-apostolic church. Writing at this dividing-line in church history, Paul developed two themes for Timothy's instruction: the first was the warning theme of apostasy: people were already moving away from Paul (1:15) and from the truth (2:18) and would increasingly move away from right-eousness (3:1ff.) and from the gospel (4:3). Within this situation Paul never promises Timothy that he will be given new truth to meet new situations or even new gifts of the Holy Spirit to gird him for new demands. Rather (and this is the second and parallel theme) he is seen as one who already possesses all the truth he will need and his task is to hold it (1:13–14), to explore 'the word of truth' (2:15), to 'continue' in the apostolic teaching and the inherited writings on the ground that 'all scripture' is God-breathed and sufficient (3:10–17) and to 'preach the word' (4:2). By implication of chapter 3, God-breathed Scripture comprises both the teaching deposited by the apostle(s) and the sacred writings inherited from the past; by both implication and statement, this is the 'word' which Timothy is to preach.

The mandate for expositors

An expository ministry is the proper response to a God-breathed Scripture. It is the task of the book to which this preface has the privilege of being attached to define exposition more exactly and to explore the ramifications of expository work. Central to it all is that concern which the word 'exposition' itself enshrines: a display of what is there. In this connection we may see Timothy as a paradigm for ministry in the post-apostolic church. He already possesses that truth which is sufficient for the perfecting of the church (2 Tim. 3:17) and for evangelistic outreach to the world (4:2–5). 'All scripture' is the depository of this truth (3:16). He can call on the Holy Spirit for aid in the task of guarding what has been entrusted to him (1:14) and his responsibility is to work at the word (2:15), keep faith with it (3:14) and preach what he finds there (4:2).

The Word becoming flesh

It is into this glorious ministry that the individual preacher is caught up by the mercy and call of God. No people are so privileged as those who earn their bread by the Word of God, nor, if they consider their calling in scriptural terms, are there any so exposed to the searchings and demands of the Word. Ezekiel experienced the miracle of verbal inspiration. It was his task to 'speak my words to them'[13] and to that end he felt himself to eat an actual donation of divine words,[14] this being the nearest way in which the miracle of what was afoot could be expressed. It is because verbal inspiration is a miracle that it is capable of being caricatured as God using people as typewriters, for here our minds are baffled and hunt for models by which to domesticate the unique. But the typewriter-model is false, for the relationship between the inspiring God and the inspired prophet is personal and moral throughout. The context of this inspiration was actually to stand in the counsel of the Lord[15] – and remember that the nearer one

---

13. Ezk. 2:7; note the plural 'words'.   14. Ezk. 2:8 – 3:3.
15. Je. 23:18, 22.

comes to God the more truly human one becomes; and the consequence of this inspiration was that the prophet was called to be the first to obey the word he preached: 'Be not rebellious like that rebellious house.'[16]

'God chose my mouth,' said Peter, in Acts 15:7. It was as personal and individual as that – the intonation of voice, the characteristic way of speaking, the choice of word and phrase, all that is instantly recognizable and frequently inimitable. Preaching is a very individual art and in that sense no-one can teach anyone else: each must learn what is natural, possible and effective, neither coveting nor copying. But one thing is common to all: the individuality of preaching must be contextualized in holiness of life. As with Ezekiel, the preacher must be first to obey. We recall what is biblically commonplace, that when lists are offered of qualifications for eldership they are always job-specifications (listing the qualifications of the person) with only one job-description (what is actually to be done), namely, teaching.[17] If we return for a moment to 2 Timothy we can see this in relation to the highest title we could possibly bear, the Lord's servant (2 Tim. 2:24–25).[18] In Paul's Greek, six qualities are listed and they are as follows, in two groups of three:

> does not fight . . . kindly . . .   an apt teacher . . .
> forbearing . . .   gentleness . . . educating . . .

The Lord's servant does no injury ('does not fight') but accepts such injury as comes his way without retaliation ('forbearing'); he is gently concerned for others' good ('kindly') but unselfassertive ('gentleness') in respect of his wants or rights. He aims to teach ('an apt teacher') and plans his teaching ('educating'). There is no doubt, then, is there,

---

16. Ezk. 2:8.   17. *E.g.* 1 Tim. 3:2ff.; Tit. 1:7ff.
18. The English versions do not always represent the order of the Greek and therefore fail to express the structure of two sets of three qualities, making three pairs as above.

what such a servant is 'for'? People must see his Lord's character in his life and hear his Lord's words on his lips.

The inspired Word is always a Word which becomes flesh. At the supreme level, this means the incarnation; at the level of the inspired Scripture it meant the holy lives of the inspired writers, drawn into the divine fellowship and closeness and required to be foremost in living out the word they preached and wrote. We who are called to preach cannot honour the Word simply by becoming devotees of an expository passion, as though Holy Scripture were a word game to be solved by the weekend. Even for us too it is the case that we must take the precious from the vile if we are to be as his mouth.[19]

Preaching as answering

But the mouth of the preacher is not the only factor involved in preaching. There is also the ear of the congregation: God chose that the Gentiles should hear. Preaching becomes communication when both mouth and ear are engaged and, as we shall see, it is expository preaching which pre-eminently brings this union about.

The Gospels often record that 'Jesus answered and said'.[20] Sometimes his answers came to questions they asked,[21] but more often his answers were his response to their needs as he discerned them.[22] As preachers we must learn to follow our Lord in hearing the spoken and unspoken needs of our congregations and making our sermons true 'replies'. Sometimes this must be done by actually taking a topic or topics which are in the public mind, but always it is done by the patient exposition of the Scriptures, for in this regard the Scriptures minister at the deepest levels to the fundamental needs of the personality.

---

19. Je. 15:19.
20. Sadly this formula is often obliterated in the modern translations and one has to go back to the Authorized or preferably the Revised Version, or nowadays to the New American Standard Bible, to find it.
21. Jn. 3:5.   22. *E.g.* Jn. 3:3.

Consider two contrasting passages. In Romans 1:18–32 we have a profound diagnosis of the world and its need. We note how the stress falls throughout on knowledge and truth[23] so that it becomes plain that in all the main areas of life – philosophy, religion and ethics[24] – man has gone astray because the truth has been lost: it has been stifled (v.18), ignored (v.21), changed (v.25), limited (v.28) and discounted (v.32).

Turn now to Ephesians 4:17–24. The theme here is individual renewal: how can people become truly human? How can we find a really human life, a fulfilling experience of our humanity? Here is an answer for the person who feels lost and asks 'Who am I?' and for the unfulfilled who cries out, 'Where is life to be found?' The answer is given that we shall be fulfilled only when the lost image has been restored. But how does this happen? We see again an emphasis on the mind[25]: it is the mind which makes a person a Gentile and the new mind which makes the new man. And the Lord Jesus Christ is presented as the new learning, the truth which sets us free.

These passages are typical of many in the Bible and they illustrate a basic diagnostic reality. Man's problem is loss of the truth and man's medicine is to have the truth ministered to him.

A dominant didactic aim

In ministry within the fellowship, often our choice of subject, always our presentation, approach, wording and attitudes will be determined by our knowledge of the people we love. But the aim and content of our preaching will be determined by their actual need to be nourished and transformed, taught and fulfilled by the Word of God. So it must be – as, again, Paul said to Timothy: we must

---

23. See vv. 18, 19, 20, 21, 22, 25, 28, 32.
24. Respectively vv. 18–21, 25 and 28.
25. See vv. 17, 18, 20, 21, 23, 24.

ever be on the alert for a chance to minister whether opportunity is obviously there or not; our address must be first to the mind ('convince'), secondly to the conscience ('rebuke') and then to the will ('exhort'), but always with patience and always with teaching intent.[26]

As we remarked earlier, the New Testament has a rich vocabulary on the subject of preaching, including over one hundred distinct verbs. Of these verbs, over two-thirds are verbs of declaration, the most common being *kēryssō* (to herald) and *didaskō* (to teach). The herald acts on another's authority; the teacher acts for another's advantage. It is exactly so with the preacher: our authority is not to be seen in our manner but in our message; it is not the exercise of dictatorial powers but the declaration of an authoritative word. It is the subjective authority of the call of God exercised in the objective authority of the ministry of his Word. The herald does not proclaim 'I say so', but 'He says so'; not 'I am over you' but 'You and I are alike and equally under him'.

The teacher works to an educative plan, meeting people where they are and patiently guiding them up through God's school in which the syllabus is the Word which he caused to be written for our learning.

The outcome

We saw in our key-verse (Acts 15:7) that the choice of God includes within its scope the result which he intends to bring about: that the hearers should believe. For this reason we preach with a certainty and an expectation resting on him to do what he has said and perform what he has planned, for 'faith comes by hearing, and hearing by the word of Christ'.[27]

J. A. MOTYER

---

26. 2 Tim. 4:2.   27. Rom. 10:17.

Preface

When reading a book I have sometimes thought of the preface as material to be skipped. It resembled hymns in a badly planned service. The author inserted it as a buffer before he got down to the business of his book.

As an author, however, I regard the preface as an absolute necessity. I write this volume with no little hesitancy, and the preface permits me to file a needed disclaimer. The literature of homiletics features the names of brilliant preachers and superior teachers. One should think twice—and twice again—before nominating himself to that company.

A reader might understandably assume that anyone writing about preaching must consider himself a master of the discipline. Not so! I have preached my share of forgettable sermons. I know the agony of preparing a message and then having preached it, feeling that I knew naked nothing about the preaching art.

If I can claim any qualification, it is this: I am a good

listener. During two decades in the classroom I have evaluated nearly six thousand student sermons. My friends marvel that after listening to hundreds of fledgling preachers stumble through their first sermons, I am not an atheist. Yet while listening I have learned what goes into an effective sermon, and I think I have discovered what to do and what to avoid. As a teacher of preachers, I'm a bit like Leo Durocher. While playing baseball his batting average was not much bigger than his shirt size, but as a manager he coached a number of successful teams.

Many of my students have gone on to be effective communicators of the Word of God, and they assure me that in some small way I have had an influence on their ministries. They and I both know that rules of homiletics do not in themselves produce effective preachers. The student must carry to the task some gift and even more, an unquenchable desire to bring a passage of Scripture into contact with life. Richard Baxter once commented that he never knew a man worth anything in his ministry who lacked a desire bordering on unhappiness to see the fruit of his labor. Principles and passion must be united before much of significance occurs in the pulpit. In this book, therefore, I pass on a method to those learning to preach or to experienced people who want to brush up on the basics. Hopefully I have expressed myself clearly enough that laymen—men and women—who teach the Scriptures will benefit. Yet to this material a reader brings himself—his life, insights, maturity, imagination, and dedication. Like hydrogen and oxygen producing water, desire and instruction together make effective communicators of God's truth.

When I started teaching, I did not intend to write. All I wanted to do was find enough usable advice to provide my students a way to proceed as they prepared to preach. In desperation for something sensible to say, I read widely. Of my debt to others I can hardly say enough. For example, H. Grady Davis made a special contribution. As I was attempting to find my way, his book found me. While he might want to disown any connection with this volume, his *Design for Preaching* proved yeast for my thinking. I have drawn from myriad other sources as well—some now forgotten, but not deliberately. To those unacknowledged contributors, I plead the experience of Homer as reported by Rudyard Kipling:

> When 'Omer smote 'is bloomin' lyre,
>   He'd 'eard men sing by land an' sea;
> An' what the thought 'e might require,
>   'E went an' took—the same as me!
>
> The market-girls an' fishermen,
>   The shepherds an' the sailors, too,
> They 'eard old songs turn up again,
>   But kep' it quiet—same as you!
>
> They knew 'e stole; 'e knew they knowed.
>   They didn't tell, nor make a fuss,
> But winked at 'Omer down the road,
>   An' 'e winked back—the same as us![1]

I acknowledge my debt to scores of others. To those students who raised the questions that I was driven to answer and who told me in gentle ways when I simply did not make myself clear, I owe much more than thanks. My former colleagues at Dallas Theological Seminary contributed far more than they realize. Duane Litfin, John Reed, Mike Cocoris, Elliott Johnson, Harold Hoehner, and Zane Hodges, among others, are men who love God with their minds—and who are not hesitant to speak them. Bruce Waltke of Regent College contributed enormously to my life over twenty years and provided a model of scholarship related to life. Since all of these and others influenced me deeply, it is only fair that for weaknesses in this volume they should shoulder a large share of the blame!

Nancy Hardin deserves special mention. Not only did she

---

1. *Rudyard Kipling's Verse: 1885–1926* (Garden City, N.Y.: Doubleday, Page, 1927), p. 403.

prepare and type the manuscript, but like a vigilant sentry she guarded my time so that I could find opportunities to write.

And my wife, Bonnie! How much I owe her! Only she knows as she reads these words how much she has done for me. Only I can know the profound influence she has had on my life.

Now that the preface is written, we can be on to the task. Anyone sensitive to the Scriptures knows the awe of the ministry. Matthew Simpson in his *Lectures on Preaching* put the preacher in his place: "His throne is the pulpit; he stands in Christ's stead; his message is the word of God; around him are immortal souls; the Savior, unseen, is beside him; the Holy Spirit broods over the congregation; angels gaze upon the scene, and heaven and hell await the issue. What associations, and what vast responsibility!"[2]

2. (New York: Phillips & Hunt, 1879), p. 166.

Abbreviations

ASV   *American Standard Version.* 1901.[1]

KJV   *King James Version.* 1611.

NASB   *New American Standard Bible.* La Habra, Calif.: Lockman Foundation, 1971.

NIV   *New International Version.* East Brunswick, N.J.: New York International Bible Society, 1978.

NKJB   *New King James Bible: New Testament.* Nashville: Thomas Nelson, 1979.

Phillips   *The New Testament in Modern English.* Translated by J. B. Phillips. New York: Macmillan, 1958.

RSV   *Revised Standard Version.* New York: Division of Christian Education, National Council of the Churches of Christ in the U.S.A., 1952, 1971.

---

1. In quotations from the American Standard Version, *Jehovah* has been changed to *Yahweh*.

Chapter 1

The Case for Expository Preaching

This is a book about expository preaching, but it may
have been written for a depressed market. Not everyone
agrees that expository preaching—or any sort of preaching,
for that matter—is an urgent need of the church. The word
is out in some circles that preaching should be abandoned.
The moving finger has passed it by and now points to other
methods and ministries that are more "effective" and in tune
with the times.

The Devaluation of Preaching

To explain why preaching receives these low grades would
take us into every area of our common life. No longer re-
garded as the intellectual or even the spiritual leader in the
community, the image of the preacher has changed. Ask the
man in the pew to describe a minister, and the description

may not be flattering. According to Kyle Haselden, the pastor comes across as a "bland composite" of the congregation's "congenial, ever helpful, ever ready to help boy scout; as the darling of the old ladies and as sufficiently reserved with the young ones; as the father image for the young people and a companion to lonely men; as the affable glad-hander at teas and civic club luncheons."[1] If that pictures reality at all, while the preacher may be liked, he will certainly not be respected.

In addition, preaching takes place in an overcommunicated society. Mass media bombard us with a hundred thousand "messages" a day. Television and radio feature pitchmen delivering a "word from the sponsor" with all the sincerity of an evangelist. Within that context the preacher may sound like another huckster who, in John Ruskin's words, "plays stage tricks with the doctrines of life and death."

More important, perhaps, the man in the pulpit feels robbed of an authoritative message. Much modern theology offers him little more than holy hunches, and he suspects that the sophisticates in the pew place more faith in science texts than in preaching texts. For some preachers, therefore, fads in communication become more stimulating than the message. Multimedia presentations, filmstrips, sharing sessions, blinking lights, and up-to-date music may be symptoms of either health or disease. Undoubtedly, modern techniques can enhance communication, but on the other hand, they can substitute for the message—the startling and unusual may mask a vacuum.

Social action appeals more to a segment of the church than talking or listening. What good are words of faith, they ask, when society demands works of faith? People with this mindset judge that the apostles had things turned around when they decided, "It is not right that we should forsake the

---

1. *The Urgency of Preaching*, pp. 88–89. Note that full bibliographical information is not supplied in the footnotes for books included in the "Selective Bibliography of Works Cited." Nor is bibliographical information that is given in the text repeated in the footnotes.

Word of God to serve tables" (Acts 6:2). In a day of activism, it is more relevant to declare instead, "It is not right that we should forsake the service of tables to preach the Word of God."

The Case for Preaching

In spite of the "badmouthing" of preaching and preachers, no one who takes the Bible seriously dare count preaching out. Paul was a writer. From his pen we have most of the inspired letters of the New Testament, and heading the list of his letters is the one to the Romans. Measured by its impact on history, few documents compare with it. Yet when Paul wrote this letter to the congregation in Rome, he confessed, "I long to see you, that I may impart to you some spiritual gift to strengthen you, that is, that we may be mutually encouraged by each other's faith, both yours and mine" (1:11–12 RSV). Paul realized that some ministries simply cannot take place apart from face-to-face contact. Even the reading of an inspired letter will not substitute. "I am eager to preach the gospel to you . . . who are in Rome" (1:15 RSV). A power comes through the word preached that even the inerrant written word cannot replace.

To the New Testament writers preaching stands as the event through which God works. Peter, for example, reminded his readers that they had "been born anew, not of perishable seed but of imperishable, through the living and abiding word of God" (I Peter 1:23 RSV). How had this word come to affect their lives? "That word," Peter explained, "is the good news which was *preached* to you" (1:25). Through preaching God had redeemed them.

Moreover, Paul recounted the spiritual history of the Thessalonians who had "turned to God from idols, to serve a living and true God, and to wait for his Son from heaven" (I Thess. 1:9–10 RSV). That about-face occurred, explained the apostle, because "when you received the word of God which you heard from us, you accepted it not as the word of men but as what it actually is, the word of God, which is at work in you believers" (2:13 RSV). Preaching in Paul's mind did not consist of a man discussing religion. Instead God Himself spoke through the personality and message of a preacher to confront men and women and bring them to Himself.

All of this explains why Paul encouraged his young associate Timothy to "preach the word" (II Tim. 4:2). *Preach* means "to cry out, herald, or exhort." Preaching should so stir a man that he pours out the message with passion and fervor. Not all passionate pleading from a pulpit, however, possesses divine authority. When a preacher speaks as a herald, he must cry out "the word." Anything less cannot legitimately pass for Christian preaching.

The Need for Expository Preaching

The man in the pulpit faces the pressing temptation to deliver some message other than that of the Scriptures—a political system (either right-wing or left-wing), a theory of economics, a new religious philosophy, old religious slogans, a trend in psychology. A preacher can proclaim anything in a stained-glass voice, at 11:30 on Sunday morning, following the singing of hymns. Yet when a preacher fails to preach the Scriptures, he abandons his authority. He confronts his hearers no longer with a word from God but only with another word from men. Therefore most modern preaching evokes little more than a wide yawn. God is not in it.

God speaks through the Bible. It is the major tool of communication by which He addresses individuals today. Biblical preaching, therefore, must not be equated with "the old, old story of Jesus and His love" as though it were retelling history about better times when God was alive and well. Nor is preaching merely a rehash of ideas about God—orthodox, but removed from life. Through the preaching of the Scriptures, God encounters men and women to bring them to salvation (II Tim. 3:15) and to richness and ripeness of Christian character (II Tim. 3:16–17). Something awesome happens when God confronts an individual through preaching and seizes him by the soul.

The type of preaching that best carries the force of divine authority is expository preaching. It would be fatuous, however, to assume that everyone agrees with that statement. A poll of churchgoers who have squirmed for hours under preaching labeled as expository—but dry as corn flakes without milk—could not be expected to agree. While most preachers tip their hats to expository preaching, their practice gives them away. Since they seldom do it, they too vote no.

Admittedly, expository preaching has suffered severely in the pulpits of men claiming to be its friends. Yet not all expository preaching necessarily qualifies as either "expository" or "preaching." Regrettably the Bureau of Weights and Measures does not have a standard expository sermon encased in glass against which to compare other messages. Any manufacturer may paste the label "expository" on whatever sermon he pleases, and no Ralph Nader will correct him. In spite of damage done by imposters, genuine expository preaching has behind it the power of the living God.

What then is the real thing? What constitutes expository preaching? How does it compare or contrast with other kinds of preaching?

The Definition of Expository Preaching

Defining becomes sticky business because what we define we sometimes destroy. The small boy dissected a frog to find out what made it jump, but in learning something about the parts he destroyed its life. Preaching is a living process involving God, the preacher, and the congregation, and no definition can pretend to capture that dynamic. But we must attempt a working definition anyway.

19

Expository preaching is the communication of a biblical concept, derived from and transmitted through a historical, grammatical, and literary study of a passage in its context, which the Holy Spirit first applies to the personality and experience of the preacher, then through him to his hearers.

The Passage Governs the Sermon

What particulars of this elaborate and rather dry definition should we highlight? First, and above all, the thought of the biblical writer determines the substance of an expository sermon. In many sermons the biblical passage read to the congregation resembles the national anthem played at a football game—it gets things started but is not heard again during the afternoon. In expository preaching, as R. H. Montgomery describes it, "the preacher undertakes the presentation of particular books [of the Bible] as some men would undertake the latest best seller. The preacher seeks to bring the message of definite units of God's Word to his people."

Expository preaching at its core is more a philosophy than a method. Whether or not a man can be called an expositor starts with his purpose and with his honest answer to the question: "Do you, as a preacher, endeavor to bend your thought to the Scriptures, or do you use the Scriptures to support your thought?" This is not the same question as, "Is what you are preaching orthodox or evangelical?" Nor is it the same as, "Do you hold a high view of the Bible or believe it to be the infallible Word of God?" As important as these questions may appear in other circumstances, a passing grade in systematic theology does not qualify an individual as an expositor of the Bible. Theology may protect us from evils lurking in atomistic, nearsighted interpretations, but at the same time it may blindfold us from seeing the text. In his approach to a passage, an interpreter must be willing to reexamine his doctrinal convictions and to reject the judgments of his most respected teachers. He must make a U-turn in his own previous understandings of the Bible should these conflict with the concepts of the biblical writer.

Adopting this attitude toward Scripture demands both simplicity and sophistication. On the one hand an expositor approaches his Bible with a childlike attitude to hear again the story. He does not come to argue, to prove a point, or even to find a sermon. He reads to understand and to experience what he understands. At the same time he knows he lives not as a child but as an adult locked into presuppositions and a world view that makes understanding difficult. The Bible is not a child's storybook, but great literature that requires thoughtful response. All its diamonds do not lie exposed on the surface to be picked like flowers. Its richness is mined only through hard intellectual and spiritual spadework.

The Expositor Communicates a Concept

The definition emphasizes that the expositor communicates a concept. Some conservative preachers have been led astray by their doctrine of inspiration and a poor understanding of how language works. Orthodox theologians insist that the Holy Spirit protects the individual words of the original text. Words are the stuff from which ideas are made, they argue, and unless the words are inspired, the ideas cannot be guarded from error. While a necessary plank in the evangelical platform on biblical authority, this sometimes frustrates expository preaching. Although a preacher examines words in the text and sometimes deals with particular words in preaching, words and phrases should never become ends in themselves. Words are stupid things until linked with other words to convey meaning. In our approach to the Bible, therefore, we are primarily concerned not with what individual words mean, but with what the biblical writer means through his use of words. Putting this another way, we do not understand the concepts of a passage merely because we analyze its separate words. A word-by-word grammatical

analysis can be as pointless and boring as reading a dictionary. If an expositor aims to understand the Bible and to
communicate its message, he must do so on the level of ideas.

Francis A. Schaeffer in his book *True Spirituality* argues
that the great battle for men takes place in the realm of
thought:

> Ideas are the stock of the thought-world, and from the ideas
> burst forth all the external things; painting, music, buildings,
> the love and the hating of men in practice, and equally the
> results of loving God or rebellion against God, in the external
> world. Where a man will spend eternity depends on his reading
> or hearing the ideas, the propositional truth, the facts of the
> gospel . . . either his believing God on the basis of the content
> of the gospel or his calling God a liar. . . . The preaching of the
> gospel is ideas, flaming ideas brought to men, as God has re-
> vealed them to us in Scripture. It is not a contentless experi-
> ence internally received, but it is contentful ideas internally
> acted upon that make the difference. So when we state our
> doctrines, they must be ideas, and not just phrases. We cannot
> use doctrines as though they were mechanical pieces to a puz-
> zle. True doctrine is an idea revealed by God in the Bible and
> an idea that fits properly into the external world as it is, and
> as God made it, and to man as he is, as God made him, and
> can be fed back through man's body into his thought-world
> and there acted upon. The battle for man is centrally in the
> world of thought.[2]

The Concept Comes from the Text

The emphasis on ideas as the substance of expository
preaching does not in any way deny the importance of vocabulary or grammar. The definition goes on to explain that
in the expository sermon the idea is *derived from and transmitted through a historical, grammatical, and literary study
of a passage in its context.* This deals first with how the
preacher comes to his message and, second, with how he
communicates it. Both involve the examination of grammar,

---

2. (Wheaton, Ill.: Tyndale, 1971), pp. 121–22.

history, and literary forms. In his study the expositor searches for the objective meaning of a passage through his understanding of language, backgrounds, and the setting of the text. Then in the pulpit he presents enough of his study to the congregation so that a listener may check the interpretation for himself.

Ultimately the authority behind preaching resides not in the preacher but in the biblical text. For that reason the expositor deals largely with an explanation of Scripture, so that he focuses the listener's attention on the Bible. An expositor may be respected for his exegetical abilities and his diligent preparation, but these qualities do not transform him into a Protestant pope who speaks ex cathedra. As Henry David Thoreau wrote, "It takes two to speak the truth — one to speak, and another to hear." No truth worth knowing will be acquired without a tussle, so if a congregation grows, it must share the struggle. "To have great poets, there must be great audiences," Walt Whitman confessed. Effective expository preaching requires listeners with ears to hear. Since their souls depend upon it, a preacher must offer his hearers sufficient information to decide if what they are hearing is what the Bible actually says.

If the people in the pew must work to understand the preacher, he himself must labor to understand the writers of the Bible. *Communication* means "a meeting of meanings," and for communication to occur across an auditorium or across the centuries, those involved must share things in common — language, culture, a world view, communication forms. An expositor pulls up his chair to where the biblical authors sat. He attempts to work his way back into the world of the Scriptures to understand the message. Though he need not master all the languages, history, and literary forms of the biblical writers, an expositor should appreciate the contribution of each of these disciplines. He can become aware of the wide assortment of interpretive aids available to him for use in his study.[3] As much as possible the expositor seeks a firsthand acquaintance with the biblical writers and their ideas in context.

The Concept Is Applied to the Expositor

Our definition of expository preaching goes on to say that the truth must be applied *to the personality and experience of the preacher*. This places God's dealing with the preacher at the center of the process. As much as we might wish it otherwise, the preacher cannot be separated from the message. Who has not heard some devout brother pray in anticipation of a sermon, "Hide our pastor behind the cross so that we may see not him but Jesus only." We commend the spirit of such a prayer. Men and women must get past the preacher to the Savior. (Or perhaps the Savior must get past the preacher to the people!) Yet no place exists where a preacher may hide. Even a large pulpit cannot conceal him from view. Phillips Brooks was on to something when he described preaching as "truth poured through personality." The man affects his message. He may be mouthing a scriptural idea yet remain as impersonal as a telephone recording, as superficial as a radio commercial, or as manipulative as a "con" man. The audience does not hear a sermon, they hear a man.

Bishop William A. Quayle had this in mind when he rejected standard definitions of homiletics. "Preaching is the art of making a sermon and delivering it?" he asked. "Why no, that is not preaching. Preaching is the art of making a preacher and delivering that!" Expository preaching should develop the preacher into a mature Christian. As the expositor studies his Bible, the Holy Spirit studies him. When a man prepares expository sermons, God prepares the man. As P. T. Forsyth said, "The Bible is the supreme preacher to the preacher."

---

3. Some of these aids will be discussed in chapter 3.

Distinctions made between "studying the Bible to get a sermon and studying the Bible to feed your own soul," are misleading and false. A scholar may examine the Bible as Hebrew poetry or as a record of the births and reigns of long-dead kings and yet not be confronted by its truth. Yet no such detachment can exist for one who opens the Book as the Word of God. Before a man proclaims the message of the Bible to others, he should live with that message himself.

Regrettably, many preachers fail as Christians before they fail as preachers because they do not think biblically. A significant number of ministers—many of whom profess high regard for the Scriptures—prepare their sermons without consulting the Bible at all. While the sacred text serves as an appetizer to get a sermon underway or as a garnish to decorate the message, the main course consists of the preacher's own thought or someone else's thought warmed up for the occasion.

Even in what is billed as "expository preaching" the verses can become launching pads for the preacher's own opinions. One common recipe found in homiletical cookbooks reads something like this: "Take several theological or moral platitudes, mix with equal parts of 'dedication,' 'evangelism,' or 'stewardship,' add several 'kingdoms' or 'the Bible says,' stir in a selection of stories, add 'salvation' to taste. Serve hot on a bed of Scripture verses." Such sermons not only leave a congregation undernourished; worse, they starve the preacher. He does not grow because the Holy Spirit has nothing to feed him. William Barclay diagnosed the cause of spiritual malnutrition in a minister's life when he wrote: "The more a man allows his mind to grow slack and lazy and flabby, the less the Holy Spirit can say to him. True preaching comes when the loving heart and the disciplined mind are laid at the disposal of the Holy Spirit."[4] Ultimately God is more interested in developing messengers than messages, and since the Holy Spirit confronts men primarily through the Bible,

---

4. *A Spiritual Autobiography* (Grand Rapids: Eerdmans, 1975).

a preacher must learn to listen to God before he speaks for Him.

The Concept Is Applied to the Hearers

But not only does the Holy Spirit apply His truth to the personality and experience of the preacher, according to our definition He then applies that truth *through him to his hearers*. An expositor thinks in three areas. First, as an *exegete* he struggles with the meanings of the biblical writer. Then as a *man of God* he wrestles with how God wants to change him personally. Finally, as a *preacher* he ponders what God wants to say to his congregation.

Application gives expository preaching purpose. As a shepherd the expositor relates to the hurts, cries, and fears of his flock. Therefore he studies the Scriptures, wondering what they say to his people in grief and guilt, doubt and death. Paul reminded Timothy that the Scriptures were given to be applied. "All scripture is inspired by God," he wrote, "and is useful for teaching the faith and correcting error, for resetting the direction of a man's life and training him in good living. The scriptures are the comprehensive equipment of the man of God, and fit him fully for all branches of his work" (II Tim. 3:16–17 *Phillips*).

Dull expository preaching usually lacks creative applications. Boring sermons evoke two major complaints. First, listeners grumble, "It's always the same old thing." The preacher gives all passages the same application, or worse, no application at all. "May the Holy Spirit apply this truth to our lives," incants a speaker who does not have a ghost of a guess himself as to how his content changes people. A second negative reaction reflects that the sermon does not relate to the world directly enough to be of practical use: "It's true enough, I guess, but so what? What difference does it make?" After all, if a man or woman decides to live under the mandate of Scripture, such action will normally take place outside the church building. On the outside, people lose jobs, worry about their children, and find crabgrass invading their lawns. Seldom do normal people lose sleep over the Jebusites, the Canaanites, or the Perizzites, or even about what Abraham, Moses, or Paul has said or done. They lie awake wondering about grocery prices, crop failures, quarrels with a girlfriend, diagnosis of a malignancy, a frustrating sex life, the rat race where only rats seem to win. If the sermon does not make much difference in that world, they wonder if it makes any difference at all.

A preacher, therefore, should forget about speaking to the ages and speak to his day. An expository preacher confronts people about themselves from the Bible instead of lecturing to them from the Bible about history or archaeology. A congregation convenes as a jury not to convict Judas, Peter, or Solomon, but to judge themselves. The expositor must know his people as well as his message, and to acquire that knowledge he exegetes both the Scripture and the congregation. After all, when God speaks He addresses men and women as they are, where they are. Imagine that Paul's letters to the Corinthians had gotten lost in the mails and instead had been delivered to the Christians at Philippi. The Philippians would have puzzled over the specific problems Paul wrote about since they lived in a different situation than their brethren in Corinth. The letters of the New Testament, like the prophecies of the Old, were addressed to specific assemblies struggling with particular problems. Expository sermons today will be ineffective unless the preacher realizes that his listeners too exist at a particular address and have mindsets unique to them.

Effective application thrusts an expositor into both theology and ethics. Going from exegesis to application, a man makes a hard trip through life-related and sometimes-perplexing questions. In addition to grammatical relationships, he also explores personal and psychological relationships. How do the characters in the text relate to one another? How are they related to God? What values lie behind the choices they make? What went on in the minds of those who were involved? These questions are not directed to the "there and then," as though God dealt with men and women only back in the "once upon a time." The same questions can be asked in the "here and now." How do we relate to one another today? How does God confront us with these same issues? In what way does the modern world compare or contrast with the biblical world? Are the questions dealt with in Scripture the questions men ask today? Are they put forth in the same way or in different forms? These probings become the raw material of ethics and theology. Application tacked on to an expository sermon in an attempt to make it relevant skirts these questions and ignores the maxim of our Protestant forebears: "Doctrines must be preached practically, and duties doctrinally."

Inappropriate application can be as destructive as inept exegesis. When Satan tempted Jesus in the wilderness, he tried to achieve victory through misapplication of Scripture. The tempter whispered Psalm 91 with admirable precision: "He will give his angels charge over you to keep you in all your ways. . . . lest you dash your foot against a stone" (vv. 11–12). Then Satan reasoned, "Since you possess this strong promise, why not apply it to a leap from the temple-top and demonstrate once and for all that you are the Son of God?" In refuting the devil, Jesus did not debate the grammar of the Hebrew text. Instead He attacked the application of Psalm 91 to temple-jumping. Another passage of Scripture better fit that situation, "You shall not tempt the Lord your God."

We must preach to a world addressed by the novelist, the columnist, and the playwright. If we do not, we will have hearers who are orthodox in their heads but heretics in their conduct. Of course in preaching to a secular world we must not preach a secular word. While biblical ideas must be shaped to human experience, men and women must be called to conform to biblical truth. "Relevant sermons" may become pulpit trifles unless they relate the current situation to the eternal Word of God.

F. B. Meyer understood the awe with which a biblical preacher speaks to the issues of his age: "He is in a line of great succession. The reformers, the Puritans, the pastors of the Pilgrim fathers were essentially expositors. They did not announce their own particular opinions, which might be a matter of private interpretation or doubtful disposition, but, taking their stand on Scripture, drove home their message with irresistible effect with 'Thus saith the Lord.' "

New Concepts

Expository preaching

Definitions

Expository preaching —the communication of a biblical concept, derived from and transmitted through
> a historical,
> grammatical,
> literary study of a passage in its context,

which the Holy Spirit first applies
> to the personality and experience of the preacher,

then through him to his hearers.

Chapter 2

What's the Big Idea?

I do not appreciate opera; what is worse, I have several friends who do. Living with them makes me feel like I exist in a cultural desert, and I have taken several steps to change my condition. On occasion I have actually attended an opera. Like a sinner shamed into attending church, I have made my way to the music hall to let culture have its way in me. On most of these visits, however, I have returned home unresponsive to what the artists have tried to do.

I understand enough about opera, of course, to know that a story has been acted out with the actors singing rather than speaking their parts. Usually, though, the story line stays as vague to me as the Italian lyrics, but opera buffs tell me that the plot is incidental to the performance. Should someone bother to ask my evaluation of the opera, I would comment on the well-constructed sets, the brilliant costumes, or the heftiness of the soprano. I could render no reliable judgment on the interpretation of the music or even the dramatic impact of the performance. When I return from the music hall with a crumpled program and an assortment of random impressions, I actually do not know how to evaluate what has taken place.

When people attend church, they may respond to the preacher like a novice at the opera. They have never been told what a sermon is supposed to do. Commonly the listener reacts to the emotional highs. He enjoys the human interest stories, jots down a catchy sentence or two, and judges the sermon a success if the preacher quits on time. Important matters, such as the subject of the sermon, may escape him completely. Years ago Calvin Coolidge returned home from services one Sunday and was asked by his wife what the minister had talked about. Coolidge replied, "Sin." When his wife pressed him as to what the preacher said about sin, Coolidge responded, "I think he was against it." The truth is that many people in the pew would not score much higher than Coolidge if quizzed about the content of last Sunday's sermon. To them, preachers preach about sin, salvation, prayer, or suffering—all together or one at a time in thirty-five minutes. Judging from the uncomprehending way in which listeners talk about a sermon, it is hard to believe that they have listened to a message. Instead the responses indicate that they leave with a basketful of fragments but no adequate sense of the whole.

Unfortunately some of us learn to preach as we have listened. Preachers, like their audiences, may conceive of sermons as a collection of points that have little relationship to each other. Here textbooks designed to help the speaker may actually hinder him. Discussions of outlining usually emphasize the place of Roman and Arabic numerals along with proper indentation, but these factors, important as they are, may ignore the obvious—an outline is the shape of the sermon idea, and the parts must all be related to the whole. Three or four points not related to a more inclusive point do not make a message; they make three or four sermonettes all preached at one time. Reuel L. Howe listened to hundreds of taped sermons, held discussions with laymen, and concluded that the people in the pew "complain almost unanimously that sermons often contain too many ideas."[1] That may not be an accurate observation. Sermons seldom fail because they have too many ideas; more often they fail because they deal with unrelated ideas.

Fragmentation poses a particular danger for the expository preacher. Some expository sermons offer little more than scattered comments based on words and phrases from a passage, making no attempt to show how the various thoughts fit together. At the outset the preacher may catch the congregation's mind with some observation about life, or worse he may jump into the text with no thought about the present at all. As the sermon goes on, the preacher comments on the words and phrases in the passage with subthemes and major themes and individual words all given equal emphasis. In the conclusion, if there is one, he usually substitutes a vague exhortation for relevant application, since no single truth has emerged for him to apply. When the congregation goes back into the world, it has received no message by which to live since it has not occurred to the preacher to preach one.

A major affirmation of our definition of expository preaching, therefore, maintains that "expository preaching is the communication of a biblical concept." That affirms the obvious. A sermon should be a bullet and not buckshot. Ideally each sermon is the explanation, interpretation, or application of a single dominant idea supported by other ideas, all drawn from one passage or several passages of Scripture.

The Importance of a Single Idea

Students of public speaking and preaching have argued for centuries that effective communication demands a single theme. Rhetoricians hold to this so strongly that virtually

1. *Partners in Preaching: Clergy and Laity in Dialogue*, p. 26.

every textbook devotes some space to a treatment of the principle. Terminology may vary—central idea, proposition, theme, thesis statement, main thought—but the concept is the same: an effective speech "centers on one specific thing, a central idea."[2] This thought is so axiomatic to speech communication that some authors, such as Lester Thonssen and A. Craig Baird, almost take it for granted:

> Little need be said here about the emergence of the central theme. It is assumed that the speech possesses a clearly defined and easily determined thesis or purpose; that this thesis is unencumbered by collateral theses which interfere with the clear perception of the principal one; and that the development is of such a character as to provide for the easy and unmistakable emergence of the thesis through the unfolding of the contents of the speech.[3]

Homileticians join their voices to insist that a sermon, like any good speech, embodies a single, all-encompassing concept. Donald G. Miller, in a chapter devoted to the heart of biblical preaching, speaks clearly:

> ... any single sermon should have just one major idea. The points or subdivisions should be parts of this one grand thought. Just as bites of any particular food are all parts of the whole, cut into sizes that are both palatable and digestible, so the points of a sermon should be smaller sections of the one theme, broken into tinier fragments so that the mind may grasp them and the life assimilate them. ... We are now ready to state in simplest terms the burden of this chapter. It is this: *Every sermon should have a theme, and that theme should be the theme of the portion of Scripture on which it is based.*[4]

---

2. William Norwood Brigance, *Speech: Its Techniques and Disciplines in a Free Society*, p. 35. See also the discussions of the central idea in: Donald C. Bryant and Karl R. Wallace, *Fundamentals of Public Speaking*, 3d ed., pp. 146–48; Milton Dickens, *Speech: Dynamic Communication*, pp. 58, 254–56, 267–71; Alma Johnson Sarett, Lew Sarett, and William Trufant Foster, *Basic Principles of Speech*, p. 215.

3. *Speech Criticism: The Development of Standards for Rhetorical Appraisal*, p. 393.

4. *The Way to Biblical Preaching*, pp. 53, 55. Italics his.

From a different tradition Alan M. Stibbs adds a seconding voice: the "preacher must develop his expository treatment of the text in relation to a single dominant theme...."[5] H. Grady Davis develops his book *Design for Preaching* in support of the thesis that "a well-prepared sermon is the embodiment, the development, the full statement of a significant thought."[6] A classic statement of this concept comes from J. H. Jowett in his Yale lectures on preaching:

> I have a conviction that no sermon is ready for preaching, not ready for writing out, until we can express its theme in a short, pregnant sentence as clear as a crystal. I find the getting of that sentence is the hardest, the most exacting, and the most fruitful labour in my study. To compel oneself to fashion that sentence, to dismiss every word that is vague, ragged, ambiguous, to think oneself through to a form of words which defines the theme with scrupulous exactness—this is surely one of the most vital and essential factors in the making of a sermon: and I do not think any sermon ought to be preached or even written, until that sentence has emerged, clear and lucid as a cloudless moon.[7]

To ignore the principle that a central, unifying idea must be at the heart of an effective sermon is to push aside what students of preaching have to tell us.[8]

35

A novice may dismiss the importance of a central idea as the ploy of homiletics professors determined to press young preachers into their mold. It should be noted, therefore, that this basic fact of communication also claims sturdy biblical support. In the Old Testament, the sermons of the prophets

---

5. *Expounding God's Word: Some Principles and Methods*, p. 40.

6. P. 20.

7. *The Preacher: His Life and Work*, p. 133.

8. For example, see: Andrew W. Blackwood, *Expository Preaching for Today: Case Studies of Bible Passages*, p. 95; John A. Broadus, *On the Preparation and Delivery of Sermons*, pp. 52–56; James W. Cox, *A Guide to Biblical Preaching*, p. 61; Faris D. Whitesell and Lloyd M. Perry, *Variety in Your Preaching*, p. 75; John Wood, *The Preacher's Workshop: Preparation for Expository Preaching*, p. 32.

are called "the burden of the Lord." These proclamations were not a few "appropriate remarks" delivered because the man of God was expected to say something. Instead the prophet addressed his countrymen because he had something to say. He preached a message, complete and entire, to persuade his hearers to return to God. As a result the sermons of the prophets possessed both form and purpose. Each embodied a single theme directed toward a particular audience in order to elicit a specific response.

In the New Testament, the historian Luke presents samples of the preaching that enabled the church to penetrate the ancient world. The sermons of the apostles were without exception the proclamation of a single idea directed toward a particular audience. The conclusion of Donald R. Sunukjian about the preaching of Paul could apply equally to the sermons of every preacher in Acts: "Each of Paul's messages is centered around one simple idea or thought. Each address crystalizes into a single sentence which expresses the sum and substance of the whole discourse. Everything in the sermons either leads up to, develops, or follows from a single unifying theme."[9]

36

It should be noted that each idea receives different treatment by the apostolic preacher. In Acts 2, for instance, on the day of Pentecost Peter stood before an antagonistic audience and, to gain a hearing, preached an inductive sermon. He does not state his idea until the conclusion: "Let all the house of Israel know for certain that God has made Him both Lord and Christ—this Jesus whom you crucified" (Acts 2:36 NASB). In Acts 13, on the other hand, Paul uses a deductive arrangement. His major idea stands at the beginning of the sermon, and the points that follow amplify and support it. The statement found in verse 23 declares, "God, according to the promise, has brought to Israel a Savior, Jesus." In Acts 20, when the apostle spoke to the Ephesian elders, his structure

---

9. "Patterns for Preaching: A Rhetorical Analysis of the Sermons of Paul in Acts 13, 17, and 20," p. 176.

was both inductive and deductive. First Paul draws from his own life an example of care for the church, then he warns in verse 28, "Be on guard for yourselves and for all the flock" (NASB). Having stated that central thought, Paul goes on to explain and apply that idea to the leaders seated before him. While not all the sermons in Acts develop in the same way, each focuses on a central unifying concept.

If we preach effectively, we must know what we are about. Effective sermons major in biblical ideas brought together into an overarching unity. Having thought God's thoughts after Him, the expositor communicates and applies those thoughts to his hearers. In dependence upon the Holy Spirit, he aims to confront, convict, convert, and comfort men and women through the preaching of biblical concepts. He knows people shape their lives and settle their eternal destinies in response to ideas.

The Definition of an Idea

What do we mean by an idea? A glance at the dictionary demonstrates that defining an idea is like packaging fog. A complete answer would send us into the broad fields of philosophy, linguistics, and grammar. Webster ranges all the way from "a transcendent entity that is a real pattern of which existing things are imperfect representations" to "an entity (as a thought, concept, sensation or image) actually or potentially present to consciousness."

The word *idea* itself moved into English from the Greek word *eidō*, which means "to see" and therefore "to know." An idea sometimes enables us to see what was previously unclear. In common life when an explanation provides new insight, we exclaim, "Oh, I see what you mean!" Still another synonym for *idea* is *concept*, which comes from the verb "to conceive." Just as a sperm and egg join in the womb to produce new life, an idea begins in the mind when things ordinarily separated come together to form a unity that either did not exist or was not recognized previously.

The ability to abstract and synthesize, that is, to think in ideas, develops with maturity. Small children think in particulars. A child praying at breakfast thanks God for the milk, cereal, orange juice, eggs, bread, butter, and jelly, but an adult combines all these separate items into the single word *food*. An idea, therefore, may be considered a distillation of life. It abstracts out of the particulars of life what they have in common and relates them to each other. Through ideas we make sense out of the parts of our experience.

All ideas, of course, are not equally valid; we have good ideas and bad ideas. Bad ideas offer explanations of experience that do not reflect reality. They read into life what is not there. Often we embrace invalid ideas because they have not been clearly stated and therefore cannot be evaluated. In our culture, influenced as it is by mass media, we are bombarded by ridiculous concepts that are deliberately left vague so we will act without thinking. Years ago Marlboro cigarettes were marketed as cigarettes for sophisticated women, but Marlboro captured less than one percent of total sales. Consumer research revealed, however, that men smoke because they believe it makes them more masculine, while women smoke because they think it makes them attractive to men. As a result of these findings, the advertisers switched their campaign away from women to men and gave Marlboros a masculine image. Rugged, weather-beaten cowpunchers were portrayed smoking cigarettes as they rounded up cattle, and the theme line invited the consumer to "come to Marlboro country." Because the association of cigarettes with cowboys conveyed the idea that smoking Marlboros makes men masculine, sales jumped four hundred percent. The idea, of course, is nonsense. Medical evidence warns us that Marlboro country is a cemetery and the Marlboro man probably suffers from cancer or lung disease. Yet because the idea that "smoking makes you masculine" slipped into the mind without being clearly stated, it gained wide acceptance and boosted sales dramatically.

This is not an isolated incident. William Bryan Key, speaking about advertising, makes this unsettling statement of a Madison Avenue doctrine: "No significant belief or attitude held by any individual is apparently made on the basis of consciously perceived data." If that stands as a fundamental affirmation behind the "word from the sponsor," we should not be surprised that truth in advertising is hard to come by.

Ideas sometimes lurk in the basement of our minds like ghosts difficult to contain. At times we struggle to give ideas expression. "I know what I mean," we say, "but I just can't put it into words." Despite the difficulty of clothing thought with words, a preacher has to do it. Unless ideas are expressed in words, we cannot understand, evaluate, or communicate them. If a preacher will not—or cannot—think himself clear so that he says what he means, he has no business in the pulpit. He is like a singer who can't sing, an actor who can't act, an accountant who can't add.

The Formation of an Idea

To define an idea with "scrupulous exactness" means that we must know how ideas are formed. When reduced to its basic structure, an idea consists of only two essential elements: a subject and a complement. Both are necessary for an idea to be complete. When we talk about the subject of an idea, we mean the complete, definite answer to the question, "What am I talking about?" The term *subject* is being used here in a technical sense. For example, the subject as it is used in homiletics is not the same thing as a subject in grammar. A grammatical subject is often a single word. The subject of a sermon idea can never be only one word since it calls for the precise, full answer to the question, "What am I talking about?" While single words such as *discipleship, wit-*

nessing, *worship*, *grief*, or *love* may masquerade as subjects, they are too vague to be viable.

A subject cannot stand alone. By itself it is incomplete, and therefore it needs a complement. The complement "completes" the subject by answering the question, "What am I saying about what I am talking about?" A subject without a complement dangles as an open-ended phrase. Complements without subjects resemble automobile parts not attached to a car. An idea emerges only when the complement is joined to a definite subject.

An example of a subject is *the test of a person's character*. (To be absolutely precise the subject is, *What is the test of a person's character?*) But that phrase must be completed to have meaning. Standing by itself we do not know what the test of character is. A variety of complements could be added to this subject to form an idea. Here are a few:

The test of a person's character is what it takes to stop him.

The test of a person's character is what she would do if she were certain no one would ever find out.

The test of a person's character is like the test of an oak — how strong is he at the roots?

Each new complement tells us what is being said about the subject, and each new complement forms a different idea. Each idea can be explained, proved, or applied.

A student of preaching must search for ideas when he reads sermons or prepares sermons of his own. Davis stresses that a beginner especially must give attention to the way ideas are formed:

He must stop getting lost in the details and study the essential structure of sermons. For the time being he has to forget about the sentences, the arguments used, the quotations, the human interest stories. He has to stand off from the sermon far enough to see its shape as a whole. Stubbornly he has to ask, "What is the man really talking about, and what are the basic things he is saying about it?" This means that he must learn to distinguish between the organic structure of the idea, on the one hand, and its development on the other. It is like beginning with the skeleton in the study of anatomy.[10]

Finding the subject and complement does not start when the expository preacher begins construction of his sermon. He pursues the subject and complement when he studies his Bible. Since each paragraph, section, or subsection of Scripture contains an idea, an exegete does not understand a passage until he can state its subject and complement exactly. While other questions emerge in the struggle to understand the meaning of a biblical writer, the two—What is the author talking about? and What is he saying about what he is talking about?—are fundamental.

Examples of Forming an Idea

In some passages the subject and complement may be discovered with relative ease, while in others determining the idea stands as the major problem in Bible study. Psalm 117 provides an example of an uncomplicated thought. The psalmist urges:

Praise the Lord, all nations;
Extol him, all you people!
For his love is strong,
his faithfulness eternal.

We do not understand the psalm until we can state its subject. What is the psalmist talking about? The subject is not *praise*, which is large and imprecise. The psalmist does not tell us everything about praise. Nor is the subject *praise of God*, which is still too broad. The subject needs more limits. A precise subject is *why everyone should praise the Lord*. What then does the psalmist say about that? He has two com-

41

---

10. *Design for Preaching*, p. 27.

plements to his subject. The Lord should be praised first because His love is strong and also because His faithfulness is eternal. In this short psalm the psalmist states his naked idea, stripped of any development, but in its bare bones it has a definite subject and two complements.

Longer passages in which the idea receives extensive development can be harder to analyze for subject and complement, but the work must be done. In Hebrews 10:19–25 the author applies a previous discussion of the high-priestly work of Jesus:

> Having therefore, brethren, boldness to enter into the holy place by the blood of Jesus, by the way which he dedicated for us, a new and living way, through the veil, that is to say, his flesh; and having a great [high] priest over the house of God; let us draw near with a true heart in fulness of faith, having our hearts sprinkled from an evil conscience: and having our body washed with pure water, let us hold fast the confession of our hope that it waver not; for he is faithful that promised: and let us consider one another to provoke unto love and good works; not forsaking our own assembling together, as the custom of some is, but exhorting one another; and so much the more, as ye see the day drawing nigh. (ASV)

While many details in this passage demand explanation, a careful student will separate the branches from the trees. Until a subject emerges, it is not possible to determine the value or significance of anything else that is said. A casual reader might be tempted to state the subject as *the high priesthood of Jesus*, but that subject covers too much. The author of Hebrews does not tell his readers everything about Christ's high-priestly work in this single paragraph. Nor is he talking about *boldness to enter the holy place*, which is actually a subidea in the passage. Instead the discussion narrows to *what should happen since we can enter into God's presence with confidence and have a great high priest*. We expect then that the complements of this subject will be a series of results, and there are three. First, let us draw near to God with the assurance that comes from a cleansed heart and life; second, let us hold unswervingly to the hope we profess; and third, let us spur on one another to love and good works. Everything else in this paragraph enlarges on this subject with its complements.

In each of these passages, we determined the subject and its complement(s) to discover the structure of the idea. In order to think clearly we must constantly distinguish the structure of the idea from the way the idea develops. The effort to state the idea of a passage or of a sermon in exact words can be frustrating and irritating, but in the long run it is the most economical use of time. What is more important, you cannot get anywhere without doing it. You do not understand what you are reading unless you can clearly express the subject and complement of the section you are studying. Those who hear you do not understand what you are saying unless they can answer the basic questions: What is the preacher talking about today? What is he saying about what he is talking about? Yet Sunday after Sunday men and women leave church unable to state the preacher's basic idea because the preacher has not bothered to state it himself. When people depart in a fog, they do so at their spiritual peril.

Thinking is difficult, but it stands as the essential work of the preacher. Let there be no mistake about the nature of the task. It is often slow, discouraging, overwhelming, but when God calls men to preach, He calls them to love Him with their minds. God deserves that kind of love and so do the people to whom we minister. On a cold, gloomy morning a preacher worked on his sermon from breakfast until noon with little to show for his labor. Impatiently he laid down his pen and looked disconsolately out the window, feeling sorry for himself because his sermons came so slowly. Then there flashed into his mind a thought that had profound effect on his later ministry: your fellow Christians will spend far more time on this sermon than you will. They will come from a hundred homes. They will travel a thousand miles in the aggregate to be in the service. They will spend three hundred hours participating in the worship and listening to what you have to say. Don't complain about the hours you are spending in preparation and the agony you experience. The people deserve all you can give them.

New Concepts

Idea
Two essential elements in the statement of an idea:
    subject
    complement

Definitions

Complement—the answer to the question, What exactly am
    I saying about what I'm talking about?
Idea—a distillation of life that abstracts out of the particulars
    of experience what they have in common and relates them
    to each other.
Subject—the complete, definite answer to the question, What
    am I talking about?

45

Exercises

Determine the subject and complement in the following paragraphs:

1. A good sermon leaves you wondering how the preacher knew all about you.

Subject:_____

Complement:_____

_____

2. Today's pulpit has lost its authority because it has largely ignored the Bible as the source of its message.

Subject:_____

Complement:_____

_____

3. G. K. Chesterton once said that it is often supposed that when people stop believing in God, they believe in nothing. Alas, it is worse than that. When they stop believing in God, they believe in anything.   *Malcolm Muggeridge*

Subject:_____

Complement:_____

_____

4. A good name is more desirable than great wealth; the respect of others is better than silver or gold.

Prov. 22:1

Subject:_____

Complement:_____

_____

5. Praise the Lord, all nations;
   Extol him, all you people!
   For his love is strong,
   his faithfulness eternal.

Ps. 117

Subject:_____

Complement:_____

_____

6. Everybody needs his memories. They keep the wolf of insignificance from the door.

Subject:_____

Complement:_____

_____

7. Do not speak harshly to a man older than yourself, but advise him as you would your own father; treat the younger men as brothers and older women as you would your mother. Always treat younger women with propriety, as if they were your sisters.   *I Tim. 5:1–2*

Subject:_____

Complement:_____

_____

8. Walking is the exercise that needs no gym. It is the prescription without medicine, the weight control without diet, the cosmetic found in no drugstore. It is the tranquilizer without a pill, the therapy without a psychoanalyst, the fountain of youth that is no legend. A walk is the vacation that does not cost a cent.

Subject:_____

Complement:_____

_____

9. The nation's latest interest in astrology, brought to public attention in the 60s, is still very much alive. The American Federation of Astrologers has doubled its national membership in the last five years to upwards of four thousand, and its mysteries, as ancient as Babylonia, have even infiltrated such a "no-nonsense" place as Washington, D.C.   *New York Times*

Subject:_____

Complement:_____

_____

10. A new book, *Eating in America: A History*, has but one remark to make about the White House Kitchen: "... at the moment of writing, there is a French chef there who turns out excellent milkshakes and double hamburgers." Well, there is nothing wrong with first-class shakes and hamburgers, and the chef is Swiss, not French, but the very fact that a 512-page tome on the history of American cuisine has only that to say about White House cooking reflects an unfortunate point: the culinary reputation of the White House is dreary indeed.

What's more, the reputation is largely undeserved. In fact, the White House has had a splendid chef for the past dozen years and puts on a display of unusually fine food for visiting dignitaries. Yet the myth persists that presidents (Kennedy excepted) willfully serve their guests such homely items as chili, hot dogs, or cottage cheese and ketchup. (These foods are produced in the president's private second-floor kitchen, which should not be confused with the basement kitchen used for official entertaining.)   *Julia Childs*

Subject:_____

Complement:_____

_____

(Answers in appendix 1.)

Stages in the Development
of Expository Messages

Chapter 3

Tools of the Trade

It is difficult to think. It is more difficult to think about thinking. It is most difficult to talk about thinking about thinking. Yet that stands as the basic task of homiletics. A homiletician observes how preachers work and attempts to get inside their heads to discover what goes on there as they prepare to preach. Then he must describe the process clearly enough to make sense to a student. The assignment borders on the impossible.

Whom should a homiletician study? Certainly not every preacher. There are duffers in the pulpit as well as on the golf course, and to discover how to do something well, we usually study those who are effective in what they do. Yet well-known pulpiteers who write "how I do it" books reveal as many variations in procedure as there are authors. More baffling perhaps are the nonmethods supposedly used by some effective preachers. These ministers who "speak from a full heart" or "share" sometimes insist that while they have abandoned the rules, their sermons still hit the target. Such preaching has to be reckoned with. As professional skills go, sermon construction ranks among the most inexact when compared, say, with cooking spaghetti, removing an appendix, or flying an airplane.

How do we evaluate the assortment of approaches or explain the apparent effectiveness of sermons that appear to have behind them no method at all? More to the point, how do we derive from all of this, procedures that others may follow?

For one thing, we are concerned with expository preaching, and ministers whose preaching is shaped by the Bible possess more in common than preachers in general. In addition, expositors who claim they follow no rules usually have not analyzed how they study. Whatever we do regularly becomes our method even if we have come to it intuitively, and few effective expositors are as methodless as they sometimes claim. Furthermore, to analyze how to do something well, we are drawn to those who do it well consistently, not those who do it well now and then by chance. Clear, relevant biblical exposition does not take place Sunday after Sunday by either intuition or accident. Good expositors have systems for their study.

52

Two conclusions do emerge from the fact that expositors go about their work in different ways: (1) thinking is a dynamic process, and (2) detailed instruction about how to think may sometimes get in the way of the process. The damage instruction can do is reflected in the story of a lawyer and physician who regularly played golf together. They were evenly matched and enjoyed a keen sense of rivalry. Then one spring the lawyer's game improved so much that the doctor was losing regularly. The doctor's attempts to better his own game were unsuccessful, but then he came up with an idea. At a bookstore he bought three how-to-play-golf manuals and sent them to the lawyer for a birthday present. It wasn't long before they were evenly matched again.

Effective biblical preaching requires insight, imagination, and spiritual sensitivity, none of which comes from merely following directions. When a discussion on how to prepare an expository sermon resembles instructions on how to build a doghouse, something has gone wrong. Building the expository sermon comes nearer to erecting cathedrals than hammering together animal shelters.

But even cathedral builders have their way of doing things. While it requires a lifetime with the Scriptures and with people to do mature exposition, the apprentice needs specific help on how to begin. Knowing how others work in the Bible can be welcome assistance. To this counsel each individual must bring his own mind, spirit, and experience, and out of repeated practice in the strenuous work of thinking, he must develop his own way of working. But an awareness of how others approach the task produces confidence and contributes to a more efficient use of time and energy.

Throughout the discussion on how to develop an expository sermon, therefore, it should be kept in mind that while the stages for preparation are treated in sequence, they sometimes mix. For example, the logical time to prepare an introduction comes when the development of the entire sermon has become clear. An experienced preacher, though, sometimes stumbles across a workable lead for an introduction early in his preparation. He takes it whenever he can get it, though he may wait until near the end of his work to fit it to his sermon.

What then are the stages in the preparation of the expository sermon?

Stage
One

53

Stage 1   Choose the passage to be preached.

An old recipe for a rabbit dish starts out, "First catch the rabbit." That puts first things first. Without the rabbit there is no dish. The obvious first questions confronting the expositor are: What shall I talk about? From what passage of Scripture should I draw my sermon?

These questions need not be faced on a Tuesday morning six days before the sermon delivery. A conscientious ministry in the Scriptures depends on thoughtful planning for the entire year. A wise expositor will save time by investing time in a preaching calendar. Sometime before his year begins he will force himself to decide Sunday by Sunday, service by service, what he will preach. While all Scripture is profitable, not every Scripture possesses equal profit for a congregation at a particular time. A preacher's insight and concern will be reflected in what biblical truths he offers to his people. In his ministry the expositor serves as a builder of bridges as he endeavors to span the gulf between the Word of God and the concerns of men and women. To do this he must be as familiar with the needs of his church as he is with the content of his Bible. While he relates the Scriptures to his people's lives in many ways, none will have more importance than choosing what he will teach them throughout the year.

Thought Units

Often he will work his way chapter by chapter, verse by verse, through different books of the Bible. In making his calendar, therefore, he will read through the books several times and then divide them into portions he will expound in particular sermons. In doing this he should select the passages on natural, not forced, divisions of the material. He will not count out ten or twelve verses to a sermon as though each verse could be handled as a separate thought. Instead he will search for the biblical writer's ideas. In the New Testament letters this means that texts will usually be selected by paragraph divisions, since paragraphs delineate the building blocks of thought. The expositor will usually choose one or more of these paragraphs to expound, depending on how they relate to one another and thus to the author's idea.

Of course no divine hand fashioned our paragraph divisions. The indentions in our translations reflect the decisions of editors who have attempted to mark out shifts of thought in the original. Consequently paragraph divisions in one translation may differ from those in another. As a general rule, older translations such as the English Revised and American Standard versions tend toward longer, heavier paragraphs than do our more modern translations, which emphasize readability and eye appeal. Even the Hebrew and Greek texts reflect editorial variations in the paragraph divisions. Yet all efforts at paragraphing recognize the central principles of development and transition of thought. A diligent expositor will examine the paragraph breakdowns in both the original texts and the English translations, select the divisions of the material that seem to be the most helpful, and use these as the basis of his exposition.

If he is working within narrative sections, however, the expositor will more likely deal with a literary unit larger than a paragraph or two. For example, when exploring an episode such as David's adultery with Bathsheba, the expositor would violate the story were he to preach it a paragraph at a time. Instead he would probably take his sermon from the entire eleventh chapter of II Samuel and at least part of the twelfth, since all of this records the sin and its devastating consequences.

In poetic literature such as the psalm, a paragraph roughly equals the stanza or strophe of a poem. While a preacher may expound only a single stanza, normally he will treat the entire psalm. In selecting passages for the expository sermon, therefore, a principle to follow is this: Base the sermon on some unit of biblical thought.

Sermon Length

A second factor in choosing what to preach relates to time. A minister must preach his sermon in a limited number of minutes. While few congregations being offered biblical food, well-prepared and attractively served, will sit before their pastor with stopwatches in their heads, an honest man will not steal time not granted to him. An expositor must tailor his sermon to his time, and the cutting should be done in the study rather than the pulpit.

Even if a minister is allowed fifty to sixty minutes for his sermon, he must make choices. A diligent pastor can seldom tell his people all he has discovered about a passage, nor should he try. Whether he has thirty minutes or an hour, therefore, he must choose what to include or exclude in a particular sermon. Through experience a preacher learns how long a passage he may treat in detail. He also knows when he must settle for a bird's-eye view of a passage rather than a worm's-eye analysis. Both the units of thought and the time allowed to cover them must be considered when he selects a passage to be preached.

Topical Exposition

While many expositors work their way through biblical books, all preachers at some time or other must preach on topics. Seasons such as Easter, Thanksgiving, and Christmas require special treatment. In addition a pastor should preach on theological subjects such as the Trinity, reconciliation, the inspiration and authority of the Scriptures. He will speak to personal concerns such as guilt, grief, loneliness, jealousy, marriage and divorce. In topical exposition the preacher begins with a subject or problem and then looks for the passage, or passages, that relate to it. In dealing with a Bible doctrine he may gain help in finding material from an analytical concordance or a topical Bible. A survey of books on theology will also provide direction. Preaching on personal problems, sometimes called life-situation preaching, may prove more difficult. An expositor with a broad knowledge of his Bible will be aware of passages that feature people with problems.

He will know the temptation of Adam, the jealousy of Cain, the guilty conscience of Jacob, and the depression of Elijah. A concordance often supplies workable leads. In addition, books wrestling with moral and ethical issues from a Christian perspective will not only analyze the problem but also suggest biblical material to be considered.

Having selected the passage, however, an expositor must allow it to speak for itself. Too often a passage will not say what we expected it to say. Topical exposition faces the special danger that the preacher will read something into the scriptural account in order to read something significant out of it. He may resort to "proof texts" for favorite doctrines by ignoring completely the context in which a passage lies. He may be tempted to transform a biblical author into a modern psychologist by insisting that he say in a sermon what he never said in the Bible. Topical exposition differs from the so-called topical sermon, therefore, in that the thought of the Scripture must shape all that is said in defining and developing the topic.

Stage
Two

57

Stage 2 Study your passage and gather your notes.

The Context

First of all, a minister should relate any particular passage of Scripture to the book of which it is a part. Usually this demands reading the book several times, often in various translations. Even those who have skills in Hebrew or Greek will find it easier to map out the broad developments of an author's thought by reading it in English. Scores of different versions are available, ranging from literal, word-for-word translations like those in interlinears (where English words are placed under the Hebrew or Greek text) to colloquial versions that resort to slang or a chatty style. Different translations serve the needs of different readers. A minister can gain an impression of the sharpness and vitality of the original Hebrew or Greek by reading different kinds of translations. For example, as a study Bible he may use the New American Standard Bible, which stays close to the original but sounds stiff and wooden when read in public. For a translation that catches the dynamic equivalent of the original and concentrates on ideas rather than bare words, he may turn to the version of J. B. Phillips. A text that searches for the middle ground between allegiance to the Hebrew or Greek and a sensitive feeling for style is the New International Version. Using these translations and others, the expositor can understand the broad context of the passage.

Setting the passage within its wider framework simply gives the Bible the same chance we give the author of a paperback. What a writer means in any specific paragraph or chapter can be determined basically by fitting it into the larger argument of the book. A student does not have to investigate by himself. Introductory sections of commentaries and Old Testament and New Testament introductions usually discuss why a book was written and outline its contents. While commentators sometimes disagree on these matters, the expositor can work with their conclusions as he reads through the Scripture for himself.

Not only should the passage be placed within the broad unity of the book, but it must also be related to the immediate context. More clues to meaning come from a study of surrounding context than from an examination of details within a passage. To understand a paragraph or subsection we must explain how it develops out of what precedes it and how it relates to what follows. Would it make any difference if this particular passage were not there? What purpose does this particular passage play in the book? To understand

I Corinthians 13, for instance, we must understand that it is part of a larger unit dealing with spiritual gifts—chapters 12–14. These chapters must be studied together properly to interpret the contrast of love with spiritual gifts in chapter 13.

As you read the passage in different translations, do so with a pen in hand. Write out as precisely as possible the problems you encounter in understanding the passage. Write them all down—make yourself state them. If different translations disagree significantly, note that. It usually means that the translators look at the passage from different points of view. Try to state the differences. Perhaps what confuses you is unfamiliar background or figures of speech that are not part of your semantic grid. Asking the right questions becomes the essential step in finding answers.

Try too to state in rough fashion what you think the writer is talking about—that is, his subject—and what major assertion(s) he is making about his subject—that is, his complement. If you cannot state a subject at this point, why not? What do you need to know in order to do so?

Having placed the passage within its context, the exegete must now examine its details: the structure, vocabulary, and grammar. Here some knowledge of the original languages becomes invaluable. While the message of the Scripture may be understood in English, an understanding of Hebrew or Greek resembles receiving a program on color television. Both a black-and-white and a color set get the same picture, but color adds vividness and precision not possible in black and white.[1] An expositor need not be expert in the languages to use them with benefit, and almost anyone can use some of the available linguistic tools. Accuracy, not to speak of integrity, demands that we develop every possible skill to keep us from declaring in the name of God what the Holy Spirit never intended to convey.

---

1. I am indebted for this analogy to Harold W. Hoehner, professor of New Testament literature and exegesis at Dallas Theological Seminary.

Lexicons

At least four different aids are available to help the minister as he examines the details of his passage. First, through using a lexicon he can find definitions of a word. Major contributions of lexicons include, along with the definition of a word, root meanings, identification of some grammatical forms, a list of passages where the word occurs, classification of its uses in its various contexts, and some illustrations that help give color to the word. For the Old Testament *A Hebrew and English Lexicon of the Old Testament* by William Gesenius, Francis Brown, S. R. Driver, and Charles A. Briggs remains unsurpassed in its etymological studies and the discussion of nuances of words in different contexts. While it shares the limitations of scholarly work done at the turn of the twentieth century, it contains a treasure of material to open up the Old Testament. One technical limitation of the lexicon for those not well-equipped in Hebrew is that words are listed according to their Hebrew roots. This makes some Hebrew words quite difficult to find. An *Index to Brown, Driver & Briggs Hebrew Lexicon* compiled by Bruce Einspahr now enables a student to work in the lexicon more easily. It lists by book, chapter, and verse every Hebrew word treated in the lexicon and the page and section of the page where the word is discussed. Another more recent, though less reliable, lexicon is a *Lexicon in Veteris Testamenti Libros* by Ludwig Koehler and Walter Baumgartner.

For the New Testament *A Greek-English Lexicon of the New Testament and Other Early Christian Literature* by Walter Bauer, William F. Arndt, F. Wilbur Gingrich, and Frederick W. Danker cannot be surpassed. An *Index to the Bauer-Arndt-Gingrich Greek Lexicon,* designed for those with little or no background in Greek, has been compiled by John R. Alsop. Along with this lexicon the exegete will see coloring of Greek words through James Hope Moulton's and George Milligan's examination of *The Vocabulary of the Greek Testament Illustrated from the Papyri and Other Non-Literary*

Sources. For a grasp of how a word was used throughout the broad sweep of Greek literature from the classical era to A.D. 600, the student must turn to *A Greek-English Lexicon* by Henry George Liddell and Robert Scott. For an extended treatment of the words and concepts found in the New Testament, the ten volumes in the *Theological Dictionary of the New Testament* edited by Gerhard Kittel and Gerhard Friedrich provide discussion from a variety of theological perspectives. Speaking personally, however, I find that these volumes promise more than they deliver to an expositor. *The New International Dictionary of New Testament Theology* edited by Colin Brown provides much of the same information offered by Kittel and Friedrich but in a more usable form. Its articles are clear and brief, and nonspecialists can understand it.

Concordances

While lexicons, like dictionaries, define words, sometimes it is essential actually to study a word in the passage where it was spoken or written. To determine the meaning of words through usage, a concordance is essential. For the Old Testament Salomon Mandelkern's *Concordance on the Bible* is the best work available, but because it is written in Hebrew, those without ability in the language find it hard to use. Students who cannot read Hebrew can benefit from *The Englishman's Hebrew and Chaldee Concordance of the Old Testament* edited by George V. Wigram. Although the work is somewhat incomplete and several word studies are now inaccurate or misleading, it is the best concordance available to an English reader.

For the New Testament *A Concordance to the Greek Testament* by W. F. Moulton and A. S. Geden has no peer and is particularly helpful with tenses. It is written in Greek, however, so English readers will find *The Englishman's Greek Concordance of the New Testament* by George V. Wigram easier to use. While the Greek words are listed as in Moulton and Geden, the quotations are given from the King James (or Authorized) Version.

Obviously the New Testament authors were men of the Bible, and they reflected Old Testament thought more than pagan thought in their use of significant words. Because they studied the Septuagint, the Greek translation of the Hebrew Scriptures, an understanding of how a word was used in the Septuagint can be extremely helpful. To study the theological significance of Old Testament words used in the New Testament, a standard aid is Edwin Hatch's and Henry A. Redpath's *Concordance to the Septuagint*. Unfortunately the volume costs a prince's ransom to buy.

Probably the best English concordance is Robert Young's *Analytical Concordance to the Bible*. Relatively little value comes from merely being able to locate occurrences of English words that happen to be used in an English translation. Young's concordance does enable the reader to locate a particular verse. It also allows the English reader to recognize different Hebrew or Greek words translated by the same English word, or the variety of English words that translate a single Greek or Hebrew word. Another much-used concordance is James Strong's *Exhaustive Concordance of the Bible*. While this work is more complete—every word in the King James Version is listed—it provides less assistance in studying the usage of Hebrew or Greek words.

Grammars

But meaning does not come from words alone. Words must be understood as they are used in phrases, clauses, sentences, and paragraphs. A study of syntax examines how words combine to render meaning, and grammars assist us in that study. Not only does a grammar offer general help in describing how words are formed and put together in sentences, but those with an index to Scripture often give insight into particular passages being studied. The standard Old Testament grammar is A. E. Cowley's translation of E. Kautzsch's edition of William Gesenius's *Hebrew Grammar*. The discussions in this work are sometimes detailed and complex and therefore difficult to follow. Thomas O. Lambdin in his *Introduction to Biblical Hebrew* offers the novice a more helpful treatment of the Hebrew language.

Much more help exists for the New Testament. Probably the standard grammar has been written by F. W. Blass, A. Debrunner, and R. W. Funk, *A Greek Grammar of the New Testament*. For a more popular grammar students turn to *A Manual Grammar of the Greek New Testament* by H. E. Dana and Julius R. Mantey. More extended treatments of New Testament syntax may be found in the three volumes by James Hope Moulton, W. F. Howard, and Nigel Turner, *A Grammar of New Testament Greek,* or in A. T. Robertson's *Grammar of the Greek New Testament in Light of Historical Research*. Robertson has also written a small, practical book, *The Minister and His Greek New Testament,* which includes a chapter on "Pictures in Prepositions" that any expositor will read with profit.

Word-Study Books

Word-study books provide the exegete with insights into words and grammar. For example, A. T. Robertson serves us well with his volumes on *Word Pictures in the New Testament,* and Richard Chenevix Trench provides helpful material in *Synonyms of the New Testament*. W. E. Vine also traces many New Testament words in their contexts in his *Expository Dictionary of New Testament Words*.

Bible Dictionaries

Many questions about background and biography, as well as specific subjects, can be answered through the use of Bible dictionaries and encyclopedias. Since different reference works display different strengths, an examination of the same subject in several different encyclopedias and dictionaries enables the minister to achieve both balance and completeness. Through the use of bibliographies found at the end of each article, a reader can pursue a topic at even greater depth. J. D. Douglas used the services of 139 evangelical scholars in editing *The New Bible Dictionary.* W. F. Albright describes this as "the best one-volume dictionary in English." It provides helpful bibliographies and displays special strength in ancient Near Eastern history and archaeology. The five-volume set edited by George Arthur Buttrick and Keith Crim, *The Interpreter's Dictionary of the Bible,* supplies extensive information on many of the same subjects from a theologically liberal point of view. *The International Standard Bible Encyclopaedia,* published originally in 1915 and edited by James Orr, is being republished under the editorship of Geoffrey W. Bromiley. These volumes combine the function of a dictionary with the broader presentations of an encyclopedia. Merrill F. Unger edited a conservative *Bible Dictionary* that many pastors have found valuable. A volume that deals with the people, the cities, the culture and literature of classical Greece is *The Oxford Classical Dictionary* edited by N. G. L. Hammond and H. H. Scullard.

Commentaries

A teacher of the Scriptures needs teachers. Commentaries supply a fund of information about the meaning of words, backgrounds of passages, and the argument of a writer. As a general rule it is a less profitable investment to purchase a commentary series in entirety. A shrewder outlay of money is to select volumes on individual Bible books from several different sets. Certainly it is wise to consult an assortment of commentaries on a passage and weigh what they say against each other in determining the meaning of the biblical author.

Several bibliographies exist to guide the expositor in his selection of a library. Brevard S. Childs offers advice on building a working library on the Old Testament in his *Old Testament Books for Pastor and Teacher*. Frederick W. Danker devotes a chapter of *Multipurpose Tools for Bible Study* to an evaluation of sets and individual commentaries on the entire Bible. David M. Scholer also lists commentaries on the New Testament in chapter 15 of his *Basic Bibliographic Guide for New Testament Exegesis*. A wider treatment dealing with the building and organizing of a library is *The Minister's Library* by Cyril J. Barber. Books in this volume are evaluated primarily on the basis of how conservative they are theologically. Still another resource is unpublished bibliographies that help the exegete make the best investment of his book budget. For instance, two available from Dallas Theological Seminary are a *Bibliography for Old Testament Exegesis and Exposition* compiled by Kenneth L. Barker and Bruce K. Waltke and edited by Roy B. Zuck, and a *Bibliography for New Testament Exegesis and Exposition* compiled by S. Lewis Johnson. Another example is *Essential Books for a Pastor's Library*, annotated by the faculty of Union Theological Seminary in Virginia and available from that school.

Other Tools

For students whose background in the languages is sparse or whose effectiveness in exegesis has rusted from disuse, some help exists in getting started. Frederick W. Danker's *Multipurpose Tools for Bible Study* provides a readable and useful discussion of the interpretive tools available to the pastor, as well as practical advice on how to use them. John D. Grassmick has prepared a classroom manual for use in the basic exegesis and homiletics course taught at Dallas Theological Seminary. His *Principles and Practice of Greek Exegesis* guides the student through a step-by-step procedure in studying the book of Colossians. Any expositor will profit from exploring Robert A. Traina's treatment of *Methodical Bible Study* since the book lives up to its title in providing a way of working.

Many ministers use a legal-sized pad to record the results of their study. For passages covering only a few verses, a separate page is devoted to each verse. For larger sections a page may be used to keep track of material related to an entire paragraph. Separate sheets may also be used for notes on the idea and its development, illustrations, and possible introductions and applications.

In studying the details of the passage and placing it in its context, the expositor is already moving into the next stage.

Stage 3 As you study the passage, relate the parts to each other to determine the exegetical idea and its development.

Stage
Three

66

Linguistic and grammatical analysis must never become an end in itself, but rather should lead to a clearer understanding of the passage as a whole. The process resembles an hourglass that moves from synthesis to analysis and back to synthesis. Initially the exegete reads the passage and its context in English to understand the author's meaning. Then through analysis he tests his initial impression through an examination of the details. After that he makes a final statement of the subject and complement in the light of that study.

Throughout the analysis and synthesis, therefore, you will ask; "Exactly what is the biblical writer talking about?" When you have a possible subject, go back through the passage and relate the subject to the details. Does the subject fit the parts? Is it too broad? Is it too narrow? Is your subject an exact description of what the passage is talking about?

The Subject

The initial statement of a subject will often be too broad. To narrow it, try testing your subject with a series of definitive questions. A bit of verse tells us what those questions are:

> *I had six faithful friends,*
> *They taught me all I knew,*
> *Their names are How and What and Why,*
> *When and Where and Who.*

Applying these six questions to your proposed subject will help you be more exact. Take as a case in point James 1:5–8. "If any of you lacks wisdom, let him ask of God, who gives to all men generously and without reproach, and it will be given to him. But let him ask in faith without any doubting, for the one who doubts is like the surf of the sea driven and tossed by the wind. For let not that man expect that he will receive anything from the Lord, being a double-minded man, unstable in all his ways." (NASB)

An initial response to this paragraph might be that James is talking about *wisdom*. While wisdom emerges as a major element in the passage, it is much too broad a subject since James does not discuss everything about wisdom. Looking at the passage more closely, we find he is talking about *how to obtain wisdom,* a more precise statement of the subject. An awareness of the immediate context, however, enables us to limit the subject even further. The preceding paragraph, verses 2–4, demonstrates that joy is the proper response to trials, and our paragraph extends that discussion. Therefore, a more complete subject for James 1:5–8 would be *how to obtain wisdom in the midst of trials.* All the details in the paragraph, directly or indirectly, relate to that subject. When a proposed subject accurately describes what the author is talking about, it illuminates the detaiis of the passage; and the subject, in turn, will be illuminated by the details.

The Complement

Having isolated the subject, you must now determine the complement, or complements, that complete the subject and make it into an idea. In doing this you must become aware of the structure of the passage and distinguish between its major and supporting assertions. Often the complement becomes immediately obvious once you have stated the subject. In James 1:5–8 the complement to the subject *how to obtain wisdom in the midst of trials* is *ask God for it in faith*. A complete statement of the idea merely joins the subject with the complement: *Wisdom in trials is obtained by asking God for it in faith*. Everything else in the paragraph supports or elaborates that idea.

In some passages, particularly in the epistles, the writer weaves a tightly reasoned argument that may be analyzed through a mechanical layout. Such a layout uncovers the relationship of the dependent clauses to the independent clauses. Diagramming, a more demanding method for unraveling structure, determines the relationship of individual words within sentences. A mechanical layout or diagram may be based on either the original text or an English translation. Both bring analysis and synthesis together so that the major assertions of a passage are separate from their support. An example of a mechanical layout may be found in appendix 2.

Other Literary Forms

While the letters in the New Testament make a fundamental contribution to Christian theology, they constitute only one of many literary forms found in the Bible. In fact a great majority of people are not even aware that the Scriptures contain various types of literature such as parables, poetry, proverbs, prayers, speeches, allegories, history, laws, contracts, biography, drama, apocalyptic, and stories. To understand any of them we must be aware of the kind of literature we are reading and the conventions that are unique to it. We do not interpret poems as we do legal contracts. A parable differs significantly from a historical narrative or a love song. When working in narrative literature, an expositor will seldom have to work through a maze of complex grammatical relationships, but instead will have to derive the author's meaning from the broad study of many paragraphs. A series of different questions must be raised when trying to understand a story. A sampling of those questions might be: Who are the characters in the story and why did the author include them? Do the characters contrast with one another? How do these characters develop as the story develops? What does the setting contribute to the story? What structure holds the story together and provides its unity? How do the individual episodes fit into the total framework? What conflicts develop and how are they resolved? Why did the writer bother telling the story? What ideas lie behind the story, implied but not stated? Finally, can those ideas be stated through a subject and complement?

Much of the Old Testament is poetic in form. In those translations that print poetry as poetry and not as prose, we discover that poetry emerges as the most-used form in Old Testament literature. Even sections we ordinarily think of as prose (history, prophecy, wisdom literature) contain large amounts of poetry. Poets do not usually tell stories but instead express feelings and reflections about life and its perplexities. In Hebrew literature they communicate through parallelism that repeats, contrasts, or adds to the previous thoughts, and they use figurative language that may not be true to fact but is true to feelings. Images and figures of speech give more life and force to speech because they join the realm of experience to fact. When a farmer observes that "the land needs rain," he is true to fact, but when he says that "the earth thirsts for rain," he is true to both fact and feeling. A poet majors in structures and language to add force and depth to what he is saying. Therefore interpreting poetry raises its own set of questions. What meanings lie behind the images and figures of speech? What feelings does the poet express by his use of language? What elements of form and structure does the poet use to discipline his thought? What would be lost if the same truth were presented in prose?[2]

As you determine the writer's idea, you will also want to discern how he develops that thought in the passage. Sometimes it is helpful to paraphrase the passage in your own words. Be exact in thought, and carefully state the relationships you see within the text whether the Bible explicitly states them or not. As you write, you will change the statement of your exegetical idea to fit the parts of the passage. Never bend the passage to fit your statement of the idea.

At this point, as a result of your study, you should be able to do two things: first, to state the idea of the passage in a single sentence that combines your subject and complement; second, to outline the development of that idea from the passage.

Stage
Three

---

2. For a more detailed discussion of literary forms in the Bible, see Leland Ryken, *The Literature of the Bible* (Grand Rapids: Zondervan, 1974); and idem, "Good Reading in the Good Book," *Christianity Today*, 17 January 1975, pp. 4–7.

Bibliography

Alsop, John R. *Index to the Bauer-Arndt-Gingrich Greek Lexicon.* Grand Rapids: Zondervan, 1968.

Barber, Cyril J. *The Minister's Library.* Grand Rapids: Baker, 1974. Periodic Supplements, 1976–

Barker, Kenneth L., and Waltke, Bruce K. *Bibliography for Old Testament Exegesis and Exposition.* Edited by Roy B. Zuck. 3d ed. Dallas: Dallas Theological Seminary, 1975.

Bauer, Walter; Arndt, William F.; Gingrich, F. Wilbur; and Danker, Frederick W. *A Greek-English Lexicon of the New Testament and Other Early Christian Literature.* 2d ed. Chicago: University of Chicago, 1979.

Blass, F. W.; Debrunner, A.; and Funk, R. W. *A Greek Grammar of the New Testament.* Chicago: University of Chicago, 1961.

Bromiley, Geoffrey W., ed. *The International Standard Bible Encyclopedia.* Rev. ed. 4 vols. Grand Rapids: Eerdmans, 1979.

Brown, Colin, ed. *The New International Dictionary of New Testament Theology.* 3 vols. Exeter: Paternoster Press, 1976–1978. Vol. 3 revised, 1980. Addenda, 1983.

Buttrick, George Arthur, and Crim, Keith, eds. *The Interpreter's Dictionary of the Bible: An Illustrated Encyclopedia.* 5 vols. Nashville: Abingdon, 1962–1976.

Childs, Brevard S. *Old Testament Books for Pastor and Teacher.* Philadelphia: Westminster, 1977.

Dana, H. E., and Mantey, Julius R. *A Manual Grammar of the Greek New Testament.* New York: Macmillan, 1927.

Danker, Frederick W. *Multipurpose Tools for Bible Study.* 3d ed. St. Louis: Concordia, 1970.

Douglas, J. D., ed. *The New Bible Dictionary.* 2d revised ed. Leicester: Inter-Varsity Press, 1982.

Einspahr, Bruce, ed. *Index to Brown, Driver & Briggs Hebrew Lexicon.* Chicago: Moody, 1976.

Essential Books for a Pastor's Library. Richmond: Union Theological Seminary in Virginia, 1976.

Gesenius, William; Brown, Francis; Driver, S. R.; and Briggs, Charles A. *A Hebrew and English Lexicon of the Old Testament*. Corrected ed. Oxford: Clarendon, 1952.

Gesenius, William; Kautzsch, E.; and Cowley, A. E. *Hebrew Grammar*. 2d ed. Oxford: Clarendon, 1910.

Grassmick, John D. *Principles and Practice of Greek Exegesis*. Dallas: Dallas Theological Seminary, 1974.

Hammond, N. G. L., and Scullard, H. H., eds. *The Oxford Classical Dictionary*. 2d ed. Oxford: Clarendon, 1970.

Hatch, Edwin, and Redpath, Henry A. *A Concordance to the Septuagint and the Other Versions of the Old Testament (Including the Apocryphal Books)*. 2 vols. New York: International, 1954.

Johnson, S. Lewis. *Bibliography for New Testament Exegesis and Exposition*. Dallas: Dallas Theological Semionary, n.d.

Kittel, Gerhard, and Friedrich, Gerhard, eds. *Theological Dictionary of the New Testament*. Translated and edited by Geoffrey W. Bromiley. 10 vols. Grand Rapids: Eerdmans, 1964–1976.

Koehler, Ludwig, and Baumgartner, Walter, eds. *Lexicon in Veteris Testamenti Libros*. Leiden: Brill, 1958.

Lambdin, Thomas O. *Introduction to Biblical Hebrew*. New York: Scribner, 1971.

Liddell, Henry George, and Scott, Robert, eds. *A Greek-English Lexicon*. Edited by Henry Stuart Jones. 9th ed. Oxford: Clarendon, 1940.

Mandelkern, Salomon. *Concordance on the Bible*. Edited by Chaim Mordecai Brecher. 2 vols. New York: Shulsinger Brothers, 1955.

Moulton, James Hope; Howard, W. F.; and Turner, Nigel. *A Grammar of New Testament Greek*. 4 vols. Edinburgh: T. & T. Clark, 1906–1976.

Moulton, James Hope, and Milligan, George. *The Vocabulary of the Greek Testament Illustrated from the Papyri and Other Non-Literary Sources*. London: Hodder and Stoughton, 1930. Reprint. Grand Rapids: Eerdmans, 1976.

Moulton, W. F., and Geden, A. S. *A Concordance to the Greek Testament According to the Texts of Westcott and Hort, Tischendorf and the English Revisers*. Revised by H. K. Moulton. 5th ed. Edinburgh: T. & T. Clark, 1978.

Orr, James, ed. *The International Standard Bible Encyclopaedia*. 5 vols. Chicago: Howard-Severance, 1930. Reprint. Grand Rapids: Eerdmans, 1952.

Robertson, A. T. *A Grammar of the Greek New Testament in Light of Historical Research*. 2d ed. Nashville: Broadman, 1934.

————. *The Minister and His Greek New Testament*. New York: George H. Doran, 1923. Reprint. Grand Rapids: Baker, 1977.

————. *Word Pictures in the New Testament*. 6 vols. New York: R. R. Smith, 1930–1933. Reprint. Nashville: Broadman, 1943.

Scholer, David M. *A Basic Bibliographic Guide for New Testament Exegesis*. 2d ed. Grand Rapids: Eerdmans, 1973.

Strong, James. *The Exhaustive Concordance of the Bible . . .* New York: Hunt & Eaton, 1890. Reprint. New York: Abingdon, 1981.

Traina, Robert A. *Methodical Bible Study: A New Approach to Hermeneutics*. Ridgefield Park (?), N.J.: Robert A. Traina, 1952.

Trench, Richard Chenevix. *Synonyms of the New Testament*. 9th ed. London: Macmillan, 1880. Reprint. Grand Rapids: Eerdmans, 1948.

Unger, Merrill F. *Unger's Bible Dictionary*. 3d ed. Chicago: Moody, 1963.

Vine, W. E. *Expository Dictionary of New Testament Words*. London: Oliphants, 1979.

Wigram, George V., ed. *The Englishman's Greek Concordance of the New Testament*. 9th ed. London: Bagster, 1903. Reprint. 1981.

————, ed. *The Englishman's Hebrew and Chaldee Concordance of the Old Testament*. 5th ed. London: Bagster, 1890. Reprint. 1980.

Young, Robert. *Analytical Concordance to the Bible* ... 22d ed.
Guildford: Lutterworth Press, 1979.

New Concepts

Context
Lexicon
Concordance
Bible dictionary and encyclopedia
Mechanical layout
Diagramming
Paraphrase of a passage

Definitions

Bible dictionary and encyclopedia — contain articles on a wide variety of biblical subjects, including background of Bible books and biographies of biblical characters.

Concordance — helps determine the meaning of words through usage.

Context — the wider framework in which a passage occurs. It can be as narrow as a paragraph or chapter, but it ultimately includes the larger argument of the book.

Diagramming — shows the relationship of individual words within sentences as well as the relationship of the clauses.

Lexicon — provides definitions, root meanings, identification of some grammatical forms, a list of passages in which a word occurs, classifications of the use of a word in its various contexts, and some illustrations that help give color to a word.

Mechanical layout — shows the relationship of the dependent and independent clauses in a paragraph.

Paraphrase of a passage — states the progression of ideas in a passage in contemporary language.

Stages in the Development
of Expository Messages

1. Selecting the Passage
2. Studying the Passage
3. Discovering the Exegetical Idea
4. **Analyzing the Exegetical Idea,** page 79.
5. **Formulating the Homiletical Idea,**
   page 97.

Chapter 4

The Road from Text to Sermon

Expository sermons consist of ideas drawn from the Scriptures and related to life. To preach effectively, therefore, an expositor must be involved in three different worlds.

In his study he gathers knowledge about the Bible. Since God chose to reveal Himself within history to nations that can be located on a map, through languages described in grammars, and in cultures as developed as our own, the exegete must understand what the revelation of God meant for the men and women to whom it was originally given.

The expositor must also be aware of the currents swirling across his own times, for each generation develops out of its own history and culture and speaks its own language. A minister may stand before a congregation and deliver exegetically accurate sermons, scholarly and organized, but dead and powerless because they ignore the life-wrenching problems and questions of his hearers. Such sermons, spoken in a stained-glass voice using a code language never heard in the marketplace, dabble in great biblical concepts, but the audience feels that God belonged to the long ago and far away. Expositors must not only answer the questions our fathers asked; they must wrestle with the questions our children ask. Men or women who speak effectively for God must first struggle with the questions of their age and then speak to those questions from the eternal truth of God.

A third sphere in which a preacher must participate is his own particular world. A church has a ZIP Code and stands near Fifth and Main in some city and state. The profound issues of the Bible and the ethical, philosophical questions of our times assume different shapes in rural villages, middle-class communities, or in the ghettos of crowded cities. Ultimately the expository preacher does not address all mankind; he speaks to a particular people and calls them by name. The gift of "pastor-teacher" implies that the two functions should be joined or else an irrelevant exposition may emerge which reflects negatively on God. As one bewildered church-goer expressed it, "The trouble is that God is like the minister: we don't see him during the week, and we don't understand him on Sunday." J. M. Reu was on target when he wrote, "Preaching is fundamentally a part of the care of souls, and the care of souls involves a thorough understanding of the congregation."[1] An able shepherd knows his flock.

During the stages that follow, the preacher endeavors to bring the ancient world, the modern world, and his particular world together in the development of his sermon. In doing this the expositor does not make the Bible relevant as though he were drawing an apt illustration from an old story. Modern men and women stand under God in exactly the same position as did their counterparts in the Bible, and they hear the Word of God addressing them now. "Yahweh our God made a covenant with us in Horeb." This affirmation comes from a people being given the Decalogue a second time and living

---

1. *Homiletics: A Manual of the Theory and Practice of Preaching*, p. 129.

decades after the original giving of the Law. Yet they declared through Moses, "Yahweh our God made a covenant with *us* in Horeb. Not with our fathers did Yahweh make this covenant, but with us, who are all of us here alive this day" (Deut. 5:2–3). The community of faith, looking back at an event that had occurred at a distant time and different place, experienced that history as a present reality. God's word spoken at Sinai continued to speak to this new generation and not only related them to God but also spelled out what God expected in their relation to each other.

To expound the Scriptures so the contemporary God confronts us where we live requires that the preacher study his audience as well as his Bible. It also means that some very nuts-and-bolts questions must be asked and answered to discover how the exegetical idea and its outline can expand into a sermon. The expositor relates the Bible to life as he enters the next phase of his study.

Stage 4   Submit the exegetical idea to three developmental questions.

Exegetical study can lie on the page like soggy cereal in a bowl. What can be done to draw the snap and crackle from the idea to fashion it into a sermon vital and alive? To answer that practical question the preacher must be aware of how thought develops.

When anyone makes a declarative statement, only four things can be done to develop it. It can be restated, explained, proved, or applied. Nothing else. To recognize this simple fact opens the way to developing the sermon.

By the use of restatement, an author or speaker merely states an idea "in other words" to clarify it or to impress it on the hearer. Restatement occupies a significant place in the parallelism of Hebrew poetry. "I will sing unto Yahweh as long as I live," the psalmist informs us in Psalm 104:33; "I will sing praise to my God while I have any being" (ASV). The apostle Paul, infuriated by false teachers who substitute legalism for evangelism, uses restatement to emphasize their condemnation. "Though we, or an angel from heaven, should preach unto you any gospel other than that which we preached unto you, let him be damned! As we have said before, so say I now again, if any man preaches unto you any gospel other than that which you received, let him be damned" (Gal. 1:8–9). Jeremiah hammers home his denunciation of Babylon by restating the same thought in at least six different particulars:

> *"A sword against the Babylonians!"*
>   *declares the Lord—*
> *"against those who live in Babylon*
>   *and against her officials and wise men!*
> *A sword against her false prophets!*
>   *They will become fools.*
> *A sword against her warriors!*
>   *They will be filled with terror.*
> *A sword against her horses and chariots*
>   *and all the foreigners in her ranks!*
>   *They will become women.*
> *A sword against her treasures!*
>   *They will be plundered.*
> *A drought on her waters!*
>   *They will dry up.*
> *For it is a land of idols,*
>   *idols that will go mad with terror."*
>
> [Jer. 50:35–38 NIV]

Though restatement takes up a great deal of space in written—and especially oral—communication, for a preacher wrestling with how to enlarge his exegetical thought into a sermon, it is not of primary importance as a means of development. Three other forms of expansion, embodied in three developmental questions, prove more provocative.[2]

What Does This Mean?

One developmental question centers on explanation: *What does this mean?* Does this concept, or parts of it, need explanation? The question can be pointed at different targets. First, when directed toward the Bible it asks, "Is the author in the passage before me developing his thought primarily through explanation?" When Paul wrote to his friends at Corinth, he explained how the diversity of gifts granted to its members should work for, and not against, unity in the congregation. He sums up his idea in I Corinthians 12:11–12: "But one and the same Spirit works all these things, distributing to each one individually just as He wills. For even as the body is one and yet has many members, and all the members of the body, though they are many, are one body, so also is Christ." (NASB) In the verses surrounding this statement Paul explains the concept either by breaking it down into particulars, such as enumerating spiritual gifts, or by illustrating it through the example of a human body. By that analogy he explains that a church like a body consists of many different parts but each one contributes to the life and benefit of all. A preacher handling this section of the Corinthian letter should be aware that Paul expands his thought primarily through explanation and that explanation will probably be the major thrust of a sermon from this passage.

Second, the developmental question "What does this mean?" may also probe the audience. It takes several forms. If I simply stated my exegetical idea, would my audience respond, "What does he mean by that?" Are there elements in the passage that the biblical writer takes for granted that

---

2. H. Grady Davis has developed these questions extensively in relation to the sermon. It is beyond the scope of his book to apply them to the study of Scripture. I am indebted to him for this approach to thinking.

my audience needs explained to them? When Paul advised the Corinthians in I Corinthians 8 about meat offered to idols, idolatry and sacrifices were as familiar to his readers as shopping centers are to modern audiences. On the other hand, people today are as bewildered about the practices of idolatry as a Corinthian would be in a supermarket. Therefore a sensitive expositor realizes that when he starts to talk about "food sacrificed to idols," he must do some explaining. The passage may be misunderstood or, more damaging, misapplied unless his listeners understand the background out of which the problem developed. They must enter into the psychological, emotional, and spiritual tensions posed by eating meat previously offered in sacrifice to heathen gods. As a case in point, when Paul speaks of a weak brother, he does not mean an individual easily influenced to sin. Instead he has in mind someone who is overscrupulous and does not understand the theology of idolatry—namely, that "no idol is anything in the world" but only a creation of superstitious imaginations. In modern churches many considering themselves "strong" would be, in Paul's mind, "weak." In a treatment of this passage, therefore, what Paul took for granted with his readers requires extensive explanation today.

In I Corinthians 12:13 the apostle observes: "We were all baptized by one Spirit into one body—whether Jews or Greeks, slave or free—and we were all given the one Spirit to drink" (NIV). Here again Paul assumes what we cannot—that his readers understand the baptizing work of the Holy Spirit. A reference to "the baptism of the Holy Spirit" now causes some listeners to shift uneasily in their pews and wonder: "What does that mean?" "Isn't that an experience important to charismatics and doesn't it have something to do with speaking in tongues?" "What do people in my denomination think about it?" The minister must not ignore those responses. Instead he will anticipate them in his preparation and devote time to explaining the baptism of the Holy Spirit even though Paul did not.

One of the major battles of preaching is to attain intelligibility. Napoleon had three commands for his messengers that apply to any communicator: "Be clear! Be clear! Be clear!" Clarity does not come easily. When someone trains to be an expositor, he will probably spend three or four years in seminary. While that training prepares him to be a theologian, it sometimes gets in his way as a communicator. Theological jargon, abstract thinking, religious questions become part of the intellectual baggage that hinders preachers from speaking plainly to ordinary men and women. If the preacher entered the hospital, the television studio, the printer's shop, the locker room, or the local garage, to understand what goes on there he would persistently ask, "What do you mean?" An expert in other occupations seldom has to make himself understood to those outside his profession, but preachers are different. To religion no one is an outsider, and in fact, understanding what God says is a life-and-death matter. Therefore the expositor must anticipate what his hearers do not know and explain it to them.

The developmental question "What does that mean?," then, deals with both the passage and the people. Let an expositor imagine some courageous soul standing up in the middle of the sermon to press that question, and he will become aware of matters that must be talked about as his sermon develops.

Stage
Four
━━━
83

Is It True?

Another developmental question centers on validity. After we understand — or think we understand — what a statement means, we often ask, *Is it true?* Can I really believe it? We demand proof. An initial impulse of those who take the Bible seriously is to ignore this question and assume that an idea should be accepted as true because it comes from the Bible. Psychological acceptance seldom comes by citing the Scriptures alone, though; it must also be gained through reasoning, proofs, and illustrations.

Even the inspired writers—men of the Scriptures though they were—establish validity not only from the Old Testament but from common life as well. When Paul wanted to prove to the Corinthian congregation that he had a right to receive financial support for his ministry, he argued from both experience and the Mosaic law. In a series of rhetorical questions, he laid out his case:

> Or is it only I and Barnabas who must work for a living? Who serves as a soldier at his own expense? Who plants a vineyard and does not eat of its grapes? Who tends a flock and does not drink of the milk? Do I say this merely from a human point of view? Doesn't the law say the same thing? For it is written in the Law of Moses: "Do not muzzle an ox while it is treading out the grain." Is it about oxen that God is concerned? Surely he says this for us, doesn't he? Yes, this was written for us, because when the plowman plows and the thresher threshes, they ought to do so in the hope of sharing in the harvest. If we have sown spiritual seed among you, is it too much if we reap a material harvest from you? If others have this right of support from you, shouldn't we have it all the more? (I Cor. 9:6–12 NIV)

Paul appeals first to the logic of experience. After all, if soldiers, grape growers, shepherds, and farmers receive wages for their work, why not an apostle or teacher? Then Paul reasoned from an all-embracing principle found in the law against muzzling oxen when they tread out corn. A worker—be it beast or man—should be rewarded for work.

In using this developmental question, therefore, the expositor should note how the biblical writer validates what he has to say. The apostles used every legitimate means available to them to win assent from their audiences. When Peter preached his Pentecostal sermon, he reasoned from both experience and Scripture to prove that "God has made him both Lord and Christ—this Jesus whom you crucified!" (Acts 2:36 NASB). Jesus' miracles, the crucifixion, the resurrection, David's tomb, the phenomena of Pentecost: those verifiable events carried the weight of Peter's argument. Joel and David,

Whether you fully agree with Lewis or not, he raises a classic question, deals with it, and turns it back upon the questioner.

J. Wallace Hamilton, preaching on the providence of God, understands the serious questions that steal to the surface when we are told that we live by the providence of God every moment of our lives. He quotes an anonymous poet as he begins to deal with the doubts:

"Oh, where is the sea" the fishes cried,
As they swam the Atlantic waters through;
"We've heard of the sea and the ocean tide
And we long to gaze on its waters blue."

All around us are little fishes looking for the sea; people living, moving, having their being in an ocean of God's providence, but who can't see the ocean for the water. Maybe it's because we call it by another name. The ancient Hebrews from whom the Bible came were a religious people. They thought in religious patterns, they spoke in religious phrases, they saw in every event the direct activity of God. If it rained, it was God who sent the rain. When crops were good, it was God who yielded the increase. But that is not our language, nor the pattern of our thought. We think in terms of law—chemical, natural law. When it rains we know it is the natural condensation of vapor. When crops are good we credit it to the fertilizer. An amazing thing has happened in our way of thinking. In a world that could not for one moment exist without the activity of God, we have conditioned our minds to a way of thinking that leaves no room for him. So many of our wants are provided by what seem natural and impersonal forces that we have lost sight of the great Provider in the midst of providence. Some of us who were brought up in the country and then later moved to the city remember how easy it was to get out of the habit of returning thanks at the table, partly because the food on it came not directly from the earth but from the grocery store. A physician in New York City said, "If you ask a child where milk comes from, he won't think of saying 'From a cow.' He will say 'From a container.' "[6]

6. *Who Goes There? What and Where Is God?* (Westwood, N.J.: Revell, 1958), p. 52.

both honored by the Jewish audience as inspired prophets, were quoted as witnesses to interpret what the people experienced. In both writing and preaching, the apostles adapted themselves to their readers and listeners to establish the validity of their ideas.

When Paul addressed the intellectuals on Mars Hill, he discussed natural theology—the fact of creation and its necessary implications. Although he set forth biblical concepts, the apostle never quoted the Old Testament since the Bible meant nothing to his pagan Greek audience. Rather he supported his arguments by referring to their idols and poet-philosophers and by drawing deductions from common life. In quoting the Greek poets and philosophers, of course, Paul was not endorsing Athenian philosophy to Athenian philosophers. The Old Testament was the authority for both his major and minor assertions, as the references in the margin of the Nestle Greek text demonstrate. In quoting the pagan sources, Paul merely took advantage of insights consistent with biblical revelation and more easily accepted by his hearers.[3]

While competence requires that an expositor understand how the biblical writer establishes validity, it demands also that we wrestle with the query, "Is that true? Can I really believe that?" as it comes from our listeners. Those questions present themselves often. In a past generation, perhaps, a preacher might count on a sense of guilt lying on the fringes of a congregation's thought. Today he can count only on an attitude of questioning and doubt. Our educational system contributes to this pervasive skepticism, as does the mass media. Advertisers have created an audience of doubters who shrug off dogmatic claims and enthusiastic endorsements, no matter who makes them, as nothing more than a pitch from the sponsor.

An expositor, therefore, does well to adopt the attitude

3. N. B. Stonehouse, "The Areopagus Address," in *Paul Before the Areopagus and Other New Testament Studies* (Grand Rapids: Eerdmans, 1957), pp. 1–40.

that a statement is not true because it is in the Bible; it is in the Bible because it is true. Writing a paragraph in the pages of a leather-covered book does not make it valid. Instead the Bible states reality as it exists in the universe as God has made it and as He governs it. We would expect, therefore, the affirmations of Scripture to be reflected in the world around us. That is not to say that we establish biblical truth by studying sociology, astronomy, or archaeology, but that the valid data from these sciences seconds the truth taught in Scripture.

How does a preacher handle the developmental question "Is that true?" Imagine that you were to state to a modern congregation the mighty affirmation of Paul, "We know that in all things God works for the good of those who love him, who have been called according to his purpose" (Rom. 8:28 NIV). Most people greet that statement with raised eyebrows. "Is that true? Can we believe that?" What about the mother who was killed by a hit-and-run driver and who left behind a husband and three children? What about those Christian parents whose four-year-old son has been diagnosed as having leukemia? How is that good? What's "good" about a young missionary drowned in the muddy waters of a jungle river before he has witnessed to even one native? To work with this passage and fail to deal with questions as perplexing as these is to miss the audience completely.

Donald Grey Barnhouse works with the question of validity while expounding John 14:12: "Greater works than these shall he do; because I go unto my Father" (KJV). He used an analogy to establish the validity of his explanation:

Aboard a United States submarine in enemy waters of the Pacific, a sailor was stricken with acute appendicitis. The nearest surgeon was thousands of miles away. Pharmacist Mate Wheller Lipes watched the seaman's temperature rise to 106 degrees. His only hope was an operation. Said Lipes: "I have watched doctors do it. I think I could. What do you say?" The sailor consented. In the wardroom, about the size of a pullman drawing room, the patient was stretched out on a table beneath a floodlight. The mate and assisting officers, dressed in reversed pajama tops, masked their faces with gauze. The crew

stood by the diving planes to keep the ship steady; the cook boiled water for sterilizing. A tea strainer served as an antiseptic cone. A broken-handled scalpel was the operating instrument. Alcohol drained from the torpedoes was the antiseptic. Bent tablespoons served to keep the muscles open. After cutting through the layers of muscle, the mate took twenty minutes to find the appendix. Two hours and a half later, the last catgut stitch was sewed, just as the last drop of ether gave out. Thirteen days later the patient was back at work.

Admittedly this was a much more magnificent feat than if it had been performed by trained surgeons in a fully equipped operating room of a modern hospital. Study this analogy and you will know the real meaning of Christ's words: "Greater works than these shall he do; because I go unto my Father." For Christ, perfect God, to work directly on a lost soul to quicken and bring out of death and into life is great, but for Him to do the same thing through us is a greater work.[4]

Cynddylan Jones works to win belief with a single sentence: "You might as well try to cross the Atlantic in a paper boat," he declares, "as to get to heaven by your own good works."

C. S. Lewis comes at validity by identifying with a question that thoughtful people have about the gospel:

Here is another thing that used to puzzle me. Is it not frightfully unfair that this new life should be confined to people who have heard of Christ and been able to believe in Him? But the truth is God has not told us what His arrangements about the other people are. We do know that no man can be saved except through Christ; we do not know that only those who know Him can be saved through Him. But in the meantime, if you worried about the people outside, the most unreasonable thing you can do is to remain outside yourself. Christians are Christ's body, the organism through which He works. Every addition to that body enables Him to do more. If you want to help those outside, you must add your own little cell to the body of Christ who alone can help them. Cutting off a man's fingers would be an odd way of getting him to do more work.[5]

---

4. *Let Me Illustrate: Stories, Anecdotes, Illustrations* (Old Tappan, N.J.: Revell, 1967), pp. 358–59.

5. *Mere Christianity* (New York: Macmillan, 1952), p. 50.

Merely to ask "Is that true? Do I and my hearers believe that?" does not produce instant answers. But failing to contend with those basic questions means we will speak only to those who are already committed. Worse, because we have not been willing to live for a time on the sloping back of a question mark, we may become hucksters for a message that we do not believe ourselves. A congregation has the right to expect that we are at least aware of the problems before we offer solutions. Let the expositor work his way through the ideas in the exegetical outline and deal honestly with the question, "Would my audience accept that statement as true? If not, why not?" Let him write down the specific questions that come and, if possible, the direction of some of the answers. Before long he will discover much that he and his hearers have to think about as the sermon develops.

What Difference Does It Make?

The third developmental question relates to application. While it is essential that an expositor explain the truth of a passage, his talk is not finished until he relates that passage to the experience of his hearers. Ultimately the man or woman in the pew hopes the preacher will answer the question, *So what? What difference does it make?* All Christians have a responsibility to ask that question since they are called to live under God in the light of biblical revelation. Mortimer J. Adler classifies books as either theoretical or practical. A theoretical book may be understood and then put away on the shelf. A practical book, however, must not only be read, it must also be used. Taken in this way, the Bible is an intensely practical book since it was written to be obeyed as well as understood.

Many homileticians have not given accurate application the attention it deserves. No book has been published devoted exclusively, or even primarily, to the knotty problems raised by application.[7] As a result many church members, having listened to orthodox sermons all their lives, may be practicing heretics. Our creeds affirm the central doctrines of the faith and remind us what Christians should believe. Regrettably our creeds cannot tell us how belief in these doctrines should make us behave. That is part of a preacher's responsibility, and he must give to it diligent attention.

Basic to perceptive application is accurate exegesis. We cannot decide what a passage means to us unless first we have determined what the passage means. To do this we must sit down before the biblical writer and try to understand what he wanted to convey to his original readers. Only after we comprehend what he meant in his own terms and to his own times can we clarify what difference that should make in life today.

In order to apply a passage accurately, we must define the situation into which the revelation was originally given and then decide what a modern man or woman shares, or does not share, with the original hearers. The closer the relationship between modern man and biblical man, the more direct the application. When James writes to Jewish Christians scattered across the ancient world, "My dear brothers, take note of this: Everyone should be quick to listen, slow to speak and slow to become angry, for man's anger does not bring about the righteous life that God desires" (James 1:19–20 NIV), that counsel applies to believers in every age and in any situation since all Christians stand in that identical relationship to God and His Word.

When the correspondence between the twentieth century and the biblical passage is less direct, however, accurate application becomes more difficult. An expositor must give special attention not only to what modern men and women have in common with those who received the original revelation but also to the differences between them. As an example,

---

7. The new hermeneutic, to its credit, has embraced application as well as exegesis, but in the effort to apply the Bible creatively, it sometimes seems less concerned with understanding Scripture correctly.

Paul's many exhortations to slaves had direct application to Christian slaves in the first century and those throughout history. Many of the principles touched on in the master-slave relationship can also govern employer-employee relationships today, but to ignore the fact that modern employees are not slaves to their employers would lead to gross misapplication of these passages. For example, denouncing membership in a labor union because slaves are to "obey" their "masters" (Eph: 6:5) would be to ignore the distinction between employees and slaves.

Applying texts from the Old Testament to contemporary audiences multiplies the problems. Indeed misapplication of the Old Testament has had an embarrassing history. One unsatisfying approach lies in using these passages like a sanctified Rorschach test. The interpreter allegorizes Old Testament stories to find in them hidden meanings buried not in the text but in his own mind. Another inadequate method of handling the Old Testament uses it only as an example or illustration of New Testament doctrine. Here the authority for what is preached comes neither from the theology of the Old Testament nor from the intent of the Old Testament writer, but entirely from the expositor's theology read back into the passage. Should the expositor be challenged about his interpretation or application, he appeals not to the passage before him but to some passage in the New Testament or to a theology he assumes he and his audience share in common.

How then can we proceed as we answer the third developmental question, "So what? What difference does it make?" First, application must come from the theological purpose of the biblical writer. John Bright states the case for determining the author's intent: ". . . the preacher needs to understand not only what the text says, but also those concerns that caused it to be said, and said as it was. His exegetical labors are, therefore, not complete until he has grasped the text's theological intention. Until he has done this he cannot interpret the text, and may egregiously misinterpret it by attributing to its words an intention quite other than that of their author."[8]

We cannot understand or apply an individual passage, whether in the Old Testament or in the New, until we have studied its contexts. For instance, plunging into an analysis of a paragraph or chapter of Ecclesiastes without first gaining an appreciation for the entire book would lead to many unworthy ideas and devastating applications for people today. Only after mastering the larger passage do we find the clues for understanding what the smaller messages mean and why they were written.

Here are some questions that help us discover the author's theological purpose:

1. *Are there in the text any indications of purpose, editorial comments, or interpretive statements made about events?* In the Book of Ruth, for example, the material in chapter 4:11–21 provides a happy ending to a story with a gloomy beginning, and it affirms God's gracious direction in the lives of the characters involved. Ruth demonstrates the providence of God, and the theme of God's loving guidance, brought into focus in the conclusion, is implied throughout the book—especially in the seven prayers of blessing and in the common, ordinary way each prayer is answered. God's working is woven into the tapestry of everyday events so skillfully that at first reading we may not see Him at work at all. Only on reflection do we become aware that He was continuously acting to meet the needs and hopes of ordinary people.[9]

2. *Are theological judgments made in the text?* Comments such as "In those days Israel had no king; everyone did as he saw fit" (NIV), made twice in the book of Judges (17:6; 21:25), points to why these sordid accounts are recorded as part of Israel's history. The narrative of

---

8. *The Authority of the Old Testament* (Nashville: Abingdon, 1967; reprint ed., Grand Rapids: Baker, 1975), pp. 171–72.

9. For a splendid development of this theme and its application, see Ronald M. Hals, *The Theology of the Book of Ruth* (Philadelphia: Fortress, 1969).

David's sin with Bathsheba and his murder of Uriah flows from the pen of the historian in a matter-of-fact way until the statement in II Samuel 11:27, "But the thing David had done displeased the Lord" (NIV).

3. Narrative passages of the Bible offer special difficulties. In addition to the questions normally raised, we should ask, *Is this story given as an example or warning? If so, in exactly what way? Is this incident a norm or an exception? What limitations should be placed on it?*

4. *What message was intended for those to whom the revelation was originally given and also for subsequent generations the writer knew would read it?*

5. *Why would the Holy Spirit have included this account in Scripture?*

Other questions must be asked to apply God's Word to a contemporary audience in a situation different from that of the ones to whom the revelation was originally given.

1. *What was the communication setting in which God's Word first came? What traits do modern men and women share in common with that original audience?* For example, Deuteronomy was spoken by Moses to a new generation on the far side of the Jordan River. Members of his audience believed in Yahweh and were part of a theocracy established by God's covenant. God had entered into a treaty with them that spelled out in detail the rewards and punishments for their obedience or disobedience. All of them had come out of the wilderness with Moses, and they looked forward to entering the land God had promised to Abraham.

Christians today cannot be directly identified with that nation of Israel. The church is neither a theocracy nor a nation. We are, however, believers in Yahweh, and we are in this age the people of God, chosen by His grace to be witnesses to the world. In addition, like them, we have revelation from God that He expects us to obey.

2. *How can we identify with biblical men and women as they heard God's Word and responded—or failed to re-*

spond —in their situation? While we cannot identify with the Israelites in actually entering the land of Canaan, or with David reigning as a king in Jerusalem, or with the life-situation of a Hebrew under the law, we do share common humanity with these men and women. We can identify with their intellectual, emotional, psychological, and spiritual reactions to God and to their fellow man.

We would do well to remember J. Daniel Baumann's observation: "We are very much like the people of the ancient world. It is only in some superficial thoughts, rational beliefs, and mental moods that we are different. In all of the basic heart realities we are the same. We stand before God exactly as people in every age have stood before Him. We have all experienced David's guilt, the doubting of Thomas, Peter's denial, the falling away of Demas, perhaps even the kiss of the betrayer Judas. We are linked across the centuries by the realities and ambiguities of the human soul."[10] While it appears somewhat simplistic, we may conclude that in all the biblical accounts God confronts men and women and that we may enter into the responses people make to God and to others—as individuals, in a group, or both. That same God whose person and character never changes addresses us today in our situations, and the principles and dynamics involved in these encounters remain very much the same throughout history.

3. *What further insights have we acquired about God's dealings with His people through additional revelation?* A mystery writer often works into the first chapter of his story incidents that appear irrelevant or perplexing, but the significance of which becomes obvious in later chapters. Since the Bible stands entire and complete, no passage should be interpreted or applied in isolation from all that God has spoken.

---

10. *An Introduction to Contemporary Preaching*, p. 100.

4. *When I understand an eternal truth or guiding principle, what specific, practical applications does this have for me and my congregation?* What ideas, feelings, attitudes, or actions should it affect? Do I myself live in obedience to this truth? Do I intend to? What obstacles keep my audience from responding as they should? What suggestions might help them respond as God wants them to respond?

Ordinarily an expositor begins his study with a single passage of Scripture, and his application comes directly or by necessary implication from that passage. Should he begin with a specific need in his congregation and turn to the Bible for solutions, however, then he must decide first what passages address the questions being raised. Through an exegesis of those separate passages, then, the subject is explored. When the Bible speaks directly to these questions in a variety of texts, application and authority still come directly from Scripture. Application becomes more complex, however, when we must deal with problems biblical writers never encountered. Because Jesus Christ stands as Lord over history, Christians must respond to current ethical and political concerns from a divine perspective. We assume that the Holy Spirit has a will for such matters as abortion, test-tube babies, a life-style amid dwindling energy resources, hunger in the world, the use of technology, or government welfare programs. But the Bible cannot and does not speak to all moral or political situations, and as a result the authority for how we believe, vote, or act cannot come directly from the Scriptures. Instead it comes indirectly and depends primarily on the validity of the expositor's analysis of the issues and application of theological principles. How a question is stated and what is emphasized may produce different results. Several questions help us test the accuracy of our conclusions:

1. Have I correctly understood the facts and properly formulated the questions involved in the issue? Can those questions be stated another way so that other issues emerge?

2. Have I determined all the theological principles that must be considered? What weight do I give each principle?

3. Is the theology I espouse truly biblical, derived from disciplined exegesis and accurate interpretation of biblical passages? Proof-texting poses a special danger here. This practice finds support for a doctrine or ethical position in passages ripped from their context or interpreted without reference to the author's purpose.

Into the formation of these moral and political judgments, Alexander Miller offers helpful insight: "A valid Christian decision is compound always of both *faith* and *facts*. It is likely to be valid in the degree to which the faith is rightly apprehended and the facts are rightly measured."[11] Because our analysis of facts and our interpretation of the faith may differ, Christians disagree on ethical and political issues. Yet unless we struggle with the facts in the light of our faith, no decisions we make can accurately be called Christian.

The three developmental questions, then, prod the expositor's thinking and help him decide what must be said about his passage. The questions build on each other. We don't question the validity of ideas we do not understand, and what we don't understand or believe cannot make a positive difference in our lives. While a preacher may deal with all three questions in his sermon, usually one of the three predominates and determines the form his message will take. All of this probing leads the expositor toward his homiletical idea, which occupies him in the next stage of development.

---

11. *The Renewal of Man: A Twentieth-Century Essay on Justification by Faith* (Garden City, N.Y.: Doubleday, 1955), p. 94.

Stage 5 In light of the audience's knowledge and experience, think through the exegetical idea and state it in the most exact, memorable sentence possible.

At this point the preacher will know the direction his sermon must take and what questions must be handled in his exposition of the passage. The central idea should now be stated so that it relates to both the Bible and the audience. Advertisers know that ideas are seldom adopted as ideas but are often adopted as slogans. While the slogans of the ad man are usually little more than brightly colored bubbles, a preacher should not despise the impact of an idea well-stated. What we think means more than anything else in life—more than our social standing, more than our income, more than where we live, more than what others think about us. People are more likely to think God's thoughts after Him, to live and love and choose on the basis of biblical concepts, if those ideas are couched in memorable phrases.

When an idea is a universal principle applying to anyone at any time, then the statement of the homiletical idea can be identical to the exegetical idea. That might be the case, for instance, in Jesus' introduction to the parable of the wealthy fool. "Beware of covetousness," he cautioned, "for a man's life does not consist in the abundance of the things he possesses" (Luke 12:15 NKJB). That warning applies to citizens of any culture who set their hearts on piling up more and more of what they have enough of already. It needs no modification. When the wise man of Proverbs observes, "A soft answer turns away wrath; but a grievous word stirs up anger" (15:1), he speaks in words everyone understands. Habakkuk declares, "The righteous [person] shall live by his faith" (2:4

ASV). In saying this the prophet states one of the overarching truths of Scripture, a foundational principle in Christian experience. It needs only to be explained, not reworded.

Other exegetical ideas evolve into homiletical ideas by making them precise and personal. For example, the concept bound up in I Thessalonians 1:2–6 might be: *Paul thanked God for the Thessalonian Christians because of the results springing from their faith, hope, and love and because of the evidences of their election by God.* The preaching idea should be more simple and direct: *We can thank God for other Christians because of what they do for God and what God did for them.*

An exegetical statement of I Timothy 4:12–16 could be: *Paul exhorted Timothy to win respect for his youth by being an example in his actions and motives and by being diligent in the public ministry of the Scriptures.* A homiletical expression could be: *Young men win respect by giving attention to their personal lives and to their teaching.* Were this passage the basis of a sermon to seminary students, the proposition could be even more personal: *You can win respect for your ministry by giving attention to yourselves and to your teaching!*

Sometimes the homiletical idea will be more contemporary and less tied to the wording of the text. In expounding Romans 1:1–17, James Rose captures it with the idea: *When the effect of the gospel is all-important in the church, the force of the gospel is unstoppable in the world.* An exposition of Romans 2:1–29 might be: *Those using the law as their ladder to heaven will be left standing in hell.* In Romans 6:1–14 Paul deals with an obvious objection to the doctrine of justification by faith: such a means of declaring people righteous only encourages sin. Paul replied: *We must realize that through our union with Jesus Christ in His death and resurrection, we have died to the rule of sin and have been made alive to virtue and holiness.* A more unforgettable expression of that concept might be: *You can't live as you once did because you are no longer the person you once were.*

In Paul's discussion of meat sacrificed to idols (I Cor. 8), he counseled the Corinthians to act primarily out of love, not knowledge. A modern expositor might frame the principle: *When you think about morally indifferent matters, be flexible, in love.* The central lesson contained in the parable of the Good Samaritan could be stated: *Your neighbor is anyone whose need you see whose need you are in a position to meet.* The homiletical idea in James 1:1–16 will have a strong sound of relevance: *Your reaction to trials is a matter of life and death.* A sermon on John 3 might advance the proposition: *Even the best of us needs to be born again.*

The language used in the homiletical idea, then, should be both winsome and compelling without being sensational. Does it sparkle? Does it grab hold of a listener's mind? Can I remember it easily? Is it worth remembering? Does the language communicate effectively to modern men and women? While personal tastes enter in at this point, these questions are worth asking.

Because the homiletical idea emerges after an intensive study of a passage and extensive analysis of the audience, getting that idea and stating it creatively is the most difficult step in sermon preparation. When the idea rises in the preacher's mind "clear as a cloudless moon," he has the message to be preached.

New Concepts

Restatement
Three developmental questions
Homiletical idea

Definitions

Three developmental questions —
1. What does this mean? Explores explanation.
2. Is it true? Do I believe it? Explores validity.
3. So what? What difference does it make? Explores implications and applications.

Homiletical idea — the statement of a biblical concept in such a way that it accurately reflects the Bible and meaningfully relates to the congregation.

Restatement — the statement of an idea in different words to clarify it or to impress it upon the audience.

Exercises

Determine the subject and complement in the following exercises. In addition indicate what functional question you think each author answers.

1. The reason you can't teach an old dog new tricks is not that he is incapable of learning them. It is that he is quite content with his mastery of the old tricks, and thinks that learning new tricks is strictly for puppies. Besides, he is busy paying off the mortgage on the dog house.

   John W. Gardner

Subject:_____

Complement:_____

_____

Functional question being addressed:_____

2. The powerful voice of God warns of judgment, and the same voice expresses His compassion for those who come back to Him in His given way. We are to listen with the same intensity of awe we feel when we observe the power of water. His spoken truth is not for us to judge or edit; we are to listen, absorb, understand, and bow.

   Edith Schaeffer

Subject:_____

Complement:_____

_____

Functional question being addressed:_____

3. The best thing you can do for your golf this winter is look in a mirror. A full-length mirror is a valuable learning aid. With it you can make valuable improvement, particularly in your set-up position and putting.   *New York Times*

Subject:_____

Complement:_____

_____

Functional question being addressed:_____

4. More contagious than colds, more habit-forming than hard drugs, CB radio already affects more than 15 million Americans, and if present trends continue, will soon be as popular as sex. Once confined to truckers and other redneck types, it now affects people so intellectually discriminating that they only watch Mary Hartman on TV.

Texas Monthly

Subject:_____

Complement:_____

_____

Functional question being addressed:_____

5. A Chinese boy who wanted to learn about jade went to study with a talented old teacher. This gentleman put a piece of the stone into the youth's hand and told him to hold it tight. Then he began to talk of philosophy, men, women, the sun and almost everything under it. After an hour he took back the stone and sent the boy home. The procedure was repeated for weeks. The boy became frustrated—when would he be told about jade?—but he was too polite to interrupt his venerable teacher. Then one day when the old man put a stone into his hands, the boy cried out instantly, "That's not jade!"

Subject:_____

Complement:_____

_____

Functional question being addressed:_____

6. Rudolph Fellner reminds his classes at Carnegie-Mellon University that "melody exists only in your memory, for at any given moment you are hearing only one note of the tune." Music is a cumulative art. It is a change of sounds through time, each sound taking its meaning from those that have gone before. It is not the art for amnesiacs.

William Mayer

Subject:_____

Complement:_____

_____

Functional question being addressed:_____

7. Had security guard Frank Wills not noticed a taped door lock at the Watergate office building on June 17, 1972, we might never have known that there were those in the inner circle of the Nixon administration who lived by a code alien to the values most of us cherish. Who can say where the abuses of power might have led had there been no opportunity for these abuses to emerge into public view?

While one can argue plausibly that fundamental government policies and programs would not have changed much in terms of war and peace or the economy had the Watergate burglary not been discovered, we certainly would be farther down the road to Orwell's 1984 than we otherwise are. But because the American people had this terrifying glimpse of the abuse of government power at a time when centralized, pervasive, and intrusive government had become a general concern, we are probably farther from 1984 today than we were ten or even twenty years ago.

Elliot L. Richardson

Subject:_____

Complement:_____

_____

103

Functional question being addressed:_____

8. Work today has lost many traditional characteristics; so has play. Play has increasingly been transformed into organized sports, and sports in turn increasingly resemble work in the arduous practice and preparation, in the intense involvement of coaches and athletes (in the spirit of work), and in actual economic productivity. In a final paradox only those sports which began as work—that is, hunting and fishing—are now dominated by the spirit of play. *Sport and Society*

Subject:_____

Complement:_____

_____

Functional question being addressed:_____

(Answers in appendix 1.)

Stages in the Development
of Expository Messages

1. Selecting the Passage
2. Studying the Passage
3. Discovering the Exegetical Idea
4. Analyzing the Exegetical Idea
5. Formulating the Homiletical Idea
6. **Determining the Sermon's Purpose,**
   page 108.

Chapter 5

The Power of Purpose

Why are you preaching this sermon? That obvious question draws many inadequate answers. For example, "When 11:25 comes on Sunday morning, I'll be expected to say something. That's why I'm preaching." Or "Last week I covered Genesis 21 so this week I'll preach on Genesis 22." Sometimes total vagueness sets in: "I'm preaching this sermon because I want to give the people a challenge." Such purposes, usually implied rather than stated, produce sermons like a dropped lemon meringue pie—they splatter over everything but hit nothing very hard!

No matter how brilliant or biblical a sermon is, without definite purpose it is not worth preaching. The preacher possesses no adequate idea of why he is speaking. Imagine asking a hockey team, "What is the purpose of hockey?" All kinds of activities take place on the ice—skating, stick handling, checking, passing—but the aim of a hockey team must be to outscore the opponent. A team that does not keep this firmly in mind plays only for exercise. Why preach this sermon? A minister does an assortment of things when he faces his congregation—explains, illustrates, exhorts, exegetes, gestures, to list a few. But pity the man who fails to understand that his sermon should change lives in some specific way. A. W. Tozer speaks a perceptive word to all of us:

> There is scarcely anything so dull and meaningless as Bible doctrine taught for its own sake. Truth divorced from life is not truth in its Biblical sense, but something else and something less.... No man is better for knowing that God in the beginning created the heaven and the earth. The devil knows that, and so did Ahab and Judas Iscariot. No man is better for knowing that God so loved the world of men that He gave His only begotten Son to die for their redemption. In hell there are millions who know that. Theological truth is useless until it is obeyed. The purpose behind all doctrine is to secure moral action.[1]

Stage 6   Determine the purpose for this sermon.

The purpose states what one expects to happen in the hearer as a result of preaching this sermon. A purpose differs from the sermon idea as a target differs from the arrow; as taking a trip differs from studying a map; as baking a pie differs from reading a recipe. Whereas the idea states the truth, the purpose defines what that truth should accomplish. Henry Ward Beecher appreciated the importance of purpose when he declared: "A sermon is not like a Chinese firecracker to be fired off for the noise it makes. It is a hunter's gun, and at every discharge he should look to see his game fall." That presupposes of course that the hunter knows what he is hunting.

---

1. *Of God and Men* (Harrisburg, Pa.: Christian, 1960), pp. 26–27.

How then does an expositor determine the purpose of his sermon? He does so by discovering the purpose behind the passage he is preaching. As part of his exegesis he should ask, "Why did the author write this? What effect did he expect it to have on his readers?" No biblical writer took up his pen to jot down "a few appropriate remarks" on a religious subject. Each wrote to affect lives. When Paul wrote to Timothy, he did it "so that you may know how one ought to conduct himself in the household of God, which is the church of the living God, the pillar and support of the truth" (I Tim. 3:15 NASB).

Jude changed purposes for his letter after he sat down to write. "While I was making every effort to write you about our common salvation," he confessed, "I felt the necessity to write to you appealing that you contend earnestly for the faith which was once for all delivered to the saints" (Jude 3 NASB). John designed his account of Jesus' life to win belief in Jesus as "the Christ, the Son of God" and to secure in believers "life through his name" (John 20:31 KJV). Whole books, as well as sections within books, were written to make something happen in the thinking and actions of the readers. An expository sermon, therefore, finds its purpose in line with the biblical purposes. The expositor must first figure out why a particular passage was included in the Bible, and with this in mind decide what God desires to accomplish through the sermon in his hearers today.

The inspired Scriptures were given so that we could be "adequate, equipped for every good work" (II Tim. 3:16–17 NASB). It follows from this that an expositor should be able to put into words what quality of life or what good works should result from the preaching and hearing of his sermon. We accomplish our purpose, Paul told Timothy, through (1) teaching a doctrine, (2) refuting some error in belief or action, (3) correcting what is wrong, and (4) instructing people on the proper handling of life. Educators realize however that an effective statement of purpose goes beyond procedure and describes the observable behavior that should come as a result of teaching. A purpose statement not only describes our destination and the route we will follow to get there, but if possible tells how we can know if we have arrived. If we are not clear about where we are going, we will undoubtedly land someplace else.[2]

Roy B. Zuck has drawn up a list of verbs valuable for stating course objectives and also useful for dealing with knowledge and insight (the cognitive domain) and attitudes and action (the affective domain). This list is reproduced in table 1.

While preaching differs significantly from lecturing, stating the purpose of a sermon as though it were an instructional objective makes the sermon more direct and effective. Here are some purposes stated in measurable terms:

> The listener should understand justification by faith and be able to write out a simple definition of the doctrine. (Whether the hearers actually write out the definition or not, a preacher will be much more specific if he preaches as though they will.)

> A listener should be able to list the spiritual gifts and determine which gifts he or she has been given.

> A listener should be able to write down the name of at least one non-Christian and should resolve to pray for that individual each day for the next two weeks. (If someone does something for two weeks, they have a better chance of doing it for several months.)

> My hearers should identify one morally indifferent situation about which Christians disagree and be able to think through how to act in that situation.

---

2. For a discussion of instructional objectives helpful to any teacher, see Robert F. Mager, *Preparing Instructional Objectives*, 2d ed. (Belmont, Calif.: Fearon, 1975).

Table 1

If the goal is: Then the verb can be:	Knowledge	Insight	Attitude	Skill
	list	discriminate	determine to	interpret
	state	between	develop	apply
	enumerate	differentiate	have confidence in	internalize
	recite	between	appreciate	produce
	recall	compare	be convinced of	use
	write	contrast	be sensitive to	practice
	identify	classify	commit yourself to	study
	memorize	select	be enthusiastic	solve
	know	choose	about	experience
	trace	separate	desire to	explain
	delineate	evaluate	sympathize with	communicate
	become aware of	examine	view	assist in
	become familiar	comprehend	plan	pray about
	with	reflect on	feel satisfied	
	become cognizant of	think through	about	
	define	discern		
	describe	understand		
	recognize	discover		

The congregation should understand how God loves them and explain at least one way in which that love makes them secure.

Christians should be able to explain what people must believe to become Christians and should plan to speak to at least one person about the Lord in the coming week.

Listeners should be convinced of the necessity to study the Bible and should enroll in a church Bible class, a home Bible class, or a Bible correspondence course.

Framing purposes that describe measurable results forces the preacher to reflect on how attitudes and behavior should be altered. That in turn will enable him to be more concrete in his application of truth to life. After all, if a sermon accomplishes anything, it must accomplish something.

David Smith, a Scottish preacher, describes a sermon as "a speech concluded with a motion." One effective means of incorporating the purpose into the sermon, therefore, lies in writing out a conclusion with the purpose in mind. We concentrate our thought with greater efficiency if we know as we begin what we intend to accomplish.

New Concepts

Purpose
Measurable results

Definitions

Measurable results — the purpose of the sermon stated in terms of observable behavior.
Purpose — what one expects to happen in the hearer as a result of hearing this sermon.

113

Stages in the Development of Expository Messages

1. Selecting the Passage
2. Studying the Passage
3. Discovering the Exegetical Idea
4. Analyzing the Exegetical Idea
5. Formulating the Homiletical Idea
6. Determining the Sermon's Purpose
7. **Deciding How to Accomplish This Purpose,** page 116.
8. **Outlining the Sermon,** page 128.

Chapter 6

The Shapes Sermons Take

Samuel Johnson observed that "people need to be reminded as much as they need to be informed." In light of his counsel, let's pause for a moment to survey the territory we have traveled. Through a study of the passage, we should have determined the exegetical idea by stating clearly what the writer was talking about and what he was saying about what he was talking about. In an effort to relate the exegesis to the contemporary audience, we then probed the idea with three developmental questions: What does that mean? Is it really true? What difference does it make? From this we framed a homiletical idea that relates the biblical concept to modern men and women. In addition we established a purpose for the sermon.

At this point, therefore, we should know what we have to preach and why we are preaching it. Now the question before us is this: What must be done with this idea to carry out the purpose? What shape will the sermon assume?

Stage 7 Thinking about the homiletical idea, ask yourself how this idea should be handled to accomplish your purpose.

Basically ideas expand in line with the broad purposes of the sermon. Just as any statement we make develops through explaining, proving, or applying it, so sermon ideas too demand explanation, validation, or application.

An Idea to Be Explained

Sometimes an idea must be explained. That happens when a preacher wants his congregation to understand a doctrine of the Bible. A truth correctly comprehended carries its own application. For example, if your car comes thumping to a halt because a tire has blown out, you must change the tire. If you do not know how to change it, your greatest need is for a clear explanation. Standing beside the highway, aware of the flat tire, you will actively listen to instruction on how to fix it. Having understood the explanation you will presumably be motivated to get out the tools, jack up the car, and go about the business of trading the flat for the spare. All of this is to say that offering an audience a clear explanation of a biblical passage may be the most important contribution an expositor can make in his sermon.

One formula for sermon development that should be respected if only because it is old says: "Tell them what you are going to tell them; tell them what you are telling them; then tell them what you have told them." When our purpose requires that we explain a concept, that is splendid advice. In the introduction to such a sermon, we state the idea completely, in the body we take the idea apart and analyze it, and in the conclusion we repeat the idea again. Certainly such a development wins through clarity anything it loses in suspense.

As an example, Alexander Maclaren preached a sermon to explain Colossians 1:15–18: "Who is the image of the invisible God, the firstborn of all creation; for in him were all things created, in the heavens and upon the earth, things visible and things invisible, whether thrones or dominions or principalities or powers; all things have been created through him, and unto him; and he is before all things, and in him all things consist. And he is the head of the body, the church: who is the beginning, the firstborn from the dead; that in all things he might have the preeminence." (ASV)

Within the sermon Maclaren says, "My business is not so much to try to prove Paul's words as to explain them, and then press them home." His subject is *why Jesus Christ is supreme over all creatures in everything*, and his complement is *because of his relation to God, to the creation, and to the church*. In developing this idea through explanation, Maclaren purposes to motivate Christians to make Christ preeminent in their lives.

How then does he go about the sermon? He offers his idea twice in the introduction. "Christ," he declares, "fills the space between God and man. There is no need for a crowd of shadowy beings to link heaven with earth. Jesus Christ lays His hand upon both. He is the head and fountain of life to His church. Therefore, He is first in all things to be listened to, loved, and worshipped by men." The entire sermon will say nothing more than that. In the next paragraph Maclaren presents the idea in an abbreviated form a second time: "There are here three grand conceptions of Christ's relations. We have Christ and God, Christ and the creation, Christ and the church, and built upon all these, the triumphant proclamation of His supremacy over all creatures in all respects."

In the body of the sermon, Maclaren explains what those relationships involve. Reduced to its outline, the sermon proceeds in this way:

I. The relation of Christ to God is that He is "the image of the invisible God" (Col. 1:15).
   A. God in Himself is inconceivable and unapproachable.
   B. Christ is the perfect manifestation and image of God.
      1. In Him the invisible becomes visible.
      2. He alone provides certitude firm enough for us to find sustaining power against life's trials.

II. The relation of Christ to creation is that He is "the first-born of all creation" (Col. 1:15–17).
   A. Christ is the agent of all creation, and the phrases Paul used imply priority of existence and supremacy over everything.
   B. Christ sustains a variety of relations to the universe; this is developed through the different prepositions Paul used.

III. The relation of Christ to His church is that He is "the head of the body" who is "the beginning, the firstborn from the dead" (Col. 1:18).

Stage Seven

118

   A. What the Word of God before the incarnation was to the universe, so is the incarnate Christ to His church. He is the "firstborn" to both.
   B. As "the head of the body," He is the source and center of the church's life.
   C. As the "beginning" of the church through His resurrection, He is the power by which the church began and by which we will be raised.

Conclusion: "The apostle concludes that in all things Christ is first—and all things are, that he *may* be first. Whether in nature or in grace, the preeminence is absolute and supreme. . . . So the question of questions for us all is, 'What think ye of Christ?' . . . Is he *anything* to us but a name? . . . Happy are we if we give Jesus the preeminence, and if our hearts set 'Him first, Him last, Him midst and without end.' "[1]

---

1. An outline is not a sermon. To read this sermon with its supporting material, see Faris D. Whitesell, ed., *Great Expository Sermons*, pp. 68–77.

In this entire sermon Maclaren does little else but answer the question, What does this passage mean?

A Proposition to Be Proved

Sermons take other forms, however, and sometimes an idea requires not explanation but proof. When this is the case, the idea appears in the introduction, but as a proposition the preacher will defend. The developmental question producing this type of sermon demands validation: Is that true? Why should I believe it? Because the stance of the preacher resembles a debater, the points become *reasons* or *proofs* for his idea.

An example of a sermon in which a proposition is proved can be taken from I Corinthians 15:12–19, where Paul argues for the resurrection of the body. In the context Paul has contended that the Corinthians cannot believe that Jesus rose from the dead and continue to maintain that there is no such thing as resurrection. A sermon from verses 12–19 will defend the proposition, *The Christian faith is worthless unless Christians rise from the dead*. The preacher aims to convince his hearers that the doctrine of resurrection lies at the center of Christianity. The idea is stated in the introduction, and the major points defend it as a series of arguments. In outline form the sermon looks like this:

I. If Christians do not rise, the Christian faith lacks valid content (vv. 12–14).
   A. If the dead do not rise, it follows that Christ did not rise.
   B. If Christ did not rise, then the gospel is a delusion.
   C. If the gospel is a delusion, then our faith in that gospel has no substance.
   (A second reason why the Christian faith is worthless unless Christians rise . . .)

II. If Christians do not rise, the apostles are despicable liars (v. 15).

    A. Since the apostles all preached the resurrection of Jesus, which could not have taken place if there is no resurrection, then they are "false witnesses."

    B. They are guilty of the worst kind of falsehood since they gave lying testimony about God, whom they claimed raised Jesus from the dead.

(A third argument why the Christian faith is worthless without resurrection . . .)

III. If Christians do not rise, then the Christian faith is futile (vv. 16–17).

    A. If Christ's resurrection did not happen—which would be the case if there is no resurrection of the dead—then the effects ascribed to it are not valid.

    B. Christians therefore are still in their sins. A dead Savior is no Savior at all.

(A fourth argument to be considered . . .)

IV. If Christians do not rise, then Christians have no hope (vv. 18–19).

    A. If there is no resurrection, then Jesus was not raised and his death accomplished nothing.

    B. It would follow then that dead saints "have perished."

    C. Christians suffering for Christ in anticipation of life to come must be pitied. Without resurrection the hope that sustains them is only wishful thinking.

Conclusion: The resurrection of the dead stands as a crucial doctrine of Christianity. If it falls, the entire system of Christian faith crumbles with it, and the Christian gospel and its preachers offer nothing to the world. Since Christ has been raised, however, the belief in resurrection and the Christian faith rest on a strong foundation.

At first the idea explained and the idea proved appear to be identical since both sermons set forth the sermon idea in the introduction and then develop it. What must be recognized though is that the sermons expand in different directions to accomplish different purposes.

A Principle to Be Applied

A third development grows out of the question of application: So what? What difference does this make? In this type of sermon the expositor lays down a biblical principle in either his introduction or the first major point, and in the remainder of his message he explores the implications of the principle.

An outline of a sermon designed to apply a principle can be drawn from I Peter 2:11–3:9. The introduction to the sermon discusses how our attitudes determine action and then asks the question: As Christ's men and women what should our attitude be in a world that is no friend of God and grace? The purpose behind the sermon is *to have Christians develop a submissive spirit in their social relationships.* The principle to be applied appears in the first point.

I. We are to be subject for God's sake to every human institution (2:11–12, 21–25).
   A. Subjection brings glory to God (2:11–12).
   B. Christ illustrates submission even to institutions that worked evil against Him (2:21–25).
      1. He was completely innocent (v. 22).
      2. He remained silent and trusted Himself to God (v. 23).
      3. His sufferings were redemptive (vv. 24–25).
   (What difference should this principle make in daily life?)
II. This principle of adopting a submissive spirit for God's sake must govern us in our social relationships (2:13–20; 3:1–7).
   A. We are to submit for God's sake to civic leaders (2:13–17).

B. We are to submit for God's sake to our employers (2:18–20).

C. We are to submit for God's sake to our mates (3:1–7).
  1. Wives should have a submissive spirit toward their husbands (vv. 1–6).
  2. Husbands should have a submissive spirit toward their wives (v. 7).

Conclusion: "Let all be harmonious, sympathetic, brotherly, kindhearted, and humble in spirit; not returning evil for evil, or insult for insult, but giving a blessing instead; for you were called for the very purpose that you might inherit a blessing" (3:8–9 NASB).

A Subject to Be Completed

A fourth pattern presents only the subject in the introduction, not the entire idea, and the major points complete the subject. Without doubt this subject-completed form of development is the most common one, and many preachers attracted to the trite and true never vary from it.

In the hands of a skilled preacher, a sermon patterned this way can have a sense of tension and strong climax. James S. Stewart, in an exposition of Hebrews 12:22–25, provides a case study. In the introduction Stewart establishes his subject. The writer of Hebrews, he tells us, "is saying five things about our fellowship of Christian worship in the church." The purpose of the sermon is "to make us realize the riches of our heritage when we assemble in our places of worship." The subject having been stated, each point in the body helps to complete it.

I. It is a spiritual fellowship: "You are come unto Mt. Zion, the city of the living God, the heavenly Jerusalem" (v. 22). Christians have direct touch with that visible spiritual world which is the only ultimate reality.

("I pass on to the second fact our text underlines con-
cerning the fellowship of Christian worship.")

II. It is a universal fellowship: "You are come to the church
of the firstborn who are written in heaven" (v. 23). Christians are members of the greatest fellowship on earth,
the church universal.

("I pass on to the third description he gives of our fellowship in Christian worship.")

III. It is an immortal fellowship: "You are come to myriads
of angels in festal array, and to the spirits of just men
made perfect" (v. 23). When Christians are at worship,
their loved ones on the other side are near to them and
a cloud of witnesses surrounds them.

IV. It is a divine fellowship: "You are come to the God of all
who is Judge, and to Jesus the mediator of the new covenant" (vv. 23–24). In your worship, he tells them—
reaching now to the very heart of the matter—you have
come to God as revealed in Jesus.

("One other fact about our fellowship in worship he adds,
and so makes an end.")

V. It is a redeeming fellowship: "You are come to the blood
of sprinkling, that speaketh of better things than that of
Abel" (v. 24). "When our sins cry out to God for punish-
ment and vengeance, something else also happens—the
blood of Christ cries louder, overbears and silences the
very crying of our sins, and God for Christ's sake
forgives."[2]

Stewart makes no formal conclusion, but instead his final
point serves to bring the sermon to an effective close. Notice
that each separate point is related not to the previous point
but only to the subject that it completes.

---

2. The complete sermon, with its sturdy language and effective supporting
material, may be found in ibid., pp. 138–46.

A Story to Be Told

Sermons also communicate ideas if the expositor tells a biblical story with insight and imagination. Unfortunately, through some tortured reasoning we have persuaded ourselves that stories belong to children and that mature adults take their principles straight, without any sugar coating. Therefore we relegate stories to the nursery or we carry a novel with us on vacation only as a way to pass away the time.

The low marks we have given to the story must be revised upward if we observe the impact stories make upon us all. Television abounds with them—some shoddy, some shady, some shaky, some worthwhile—but TV drama attracts the audience and shapes its values. The future of our culture may depend on the stories that capture the imagination and mind of this generation and its children.

Anyone who loves the Bible must value the story, for whatever else the Bible is, it is a storybook. Old Testament theology comes packaged in narratives of men and women who go running off to set up their handmade gods, and of others who take God seriously enough to bet their lives on Him. When Jesus appeared, He came telling stories, and most of them have entered the world's folklore. In fact, so brilliant a storyteller was He that we sometimes miss the profound theology disguised in His tales of a rebellious delinquent and his insufferable brother, pious Pharisees, buried treasures, and a businessman who had an unexpected appointment with death.

Narrative preaching however does not merely repeat the details of a story like recounting a pointless, worn-out joke. Through the story the preacher communicates ideas. In a narrative sermon, as in any other sermon, a major idea continues to be supported by other ideas, but the content supporting the points is drawn directly from the incidents in the story. In other words the details of the story are woven together to make a point, and all the points develop the central idea of the sermon. Narratives seem most effective when the audience hears the story and arrives at the speaker's ideas without his stating them directly. Motion-picture director Stanley Kubrick discussed the power of the indirect idea in an interview reported in *Time*: "The essence of dramatic form is to let an idea come over people without its being plainly stated. When you say something directly, it is simply not as potent as it is when you allow people to discover it for themselves."[3] Whether the points are stated or only implied depends on the skill of the preacher, the purpose of the sermon, and the awareness of the audience. In any case the story should unfold so that listeners identify with the thoughts, motives, reactions, and rationalizations of the biblical characters, and in the process acquire insight into themselves as well.

Other Forms Sermons Take

Sermons also develop inductively, deductively, or through a combination of both. In deductive sermons the idea appears as part of the introduction and the body explains, proves, or applies it (see figure 1). The first three forms discussed in this chapter follow the deductive pattern. In an inductive arrangement, on the other hand, the introduction introduces only the first point in the sermon, then with a strong transition each new point links to the previous point until the idea emerges in the conclusion (see figure 1). Inductive sermons may also grow through a series of cumulative examples which when taken together lead to one general principle.

Inductive sermons produce a sense of discovery in listeners, as though they arrived at the idea on their own. Induction is particularly effective with indifferent or hostile

---

3. In Martha Duffy and Richard Schickle, "Kubrick's Grandest Gamble," *Time*, 15 December 1975, p. 72.

Figure 1

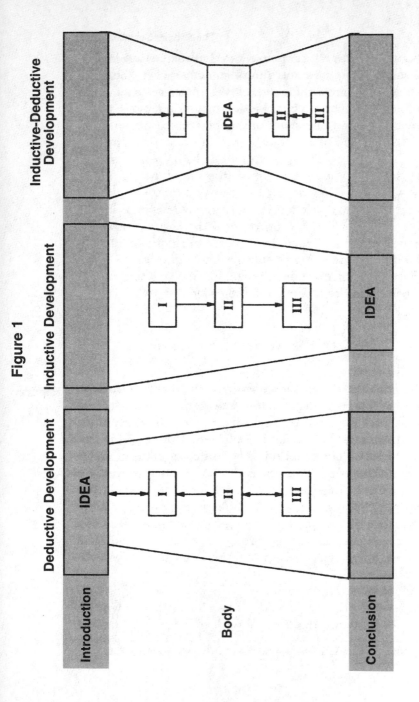

audiences likely to reject a preacher's proposition were it presented early in the sermon. When Peter addressed the throng at Pentecost—a crowd which had recently crucified Jesus— he employed an inductive approach that God used in bringing five thousand to accept Jesus as Messiah and Lord.

Induction and deduction may be combined in a sermon. The expositor develops his introduction and first point inductively, leading up to the statement of his idea. Then the remainder of the sermon proceeds deductively to explain, prove, or apply the idea. (See figure 1.)

One variation of the inductive-deductive arrangement is a problem explored. Within the introduction and first point the preacher identifies a personal or ethical problem, explores its roots, and perhaps discusses inadequate solutions. At the second point he proposes a biblical principle or approach to the problem, and throughout the remainder of the sermon, he explains, defends, or applies it. A special category of the problem-explored sermon is life-situation preaching. In the introduction the preacher discusses in personal terms a question, problem, or bewildering experience like depression or grief. He may then demonstrate that the specific case actually reflects a more general theological or philosophical problem. Finally he offers a positive biblical solution in a practical, usable manner. The sermon, therefore, becomes a bridge-building project that spans the gulf between personal needs on one side and scriptural truth on the other.

Sermons can assume many forms, and those we have surveyed should be considered not exhaustive but suggestive. The shoe must not tell the foot how to grow; therefore ideas and purposes should be allowed to take their own shape in the preacher's mind. To test a form at least two questions should be asked: (1) Does this development communicate what the passage teaches? (2) Will it accomplish my purpose with this audience? If a form communicates the message, by all means use it; if it gets in the way, devise a form more in keeping with the idea and purpose of the Scripture.

Stage 8   Having decided how the idea must be developed to accomplish your purpose, outline the sermon.

When an architect designs a building, he begins with a concept derived from function (what the building is to do) and form (how the building will look). To construct the building, the architect turns his idea into a blueprint showing in detail how the concept will translate into steel, stone, and glass.

The preacher, having derived a concept from biblical data and audience need, must now fashion a blueprint, the outline of his sermon. While content may exist without form, structure provides a sermon with a sense of order, unity, and progress. Certainly no sermon ever failed because it possessed a strong outline.

An outline therefore serves at least four purposes. First, it clarifies in the speaker's eye and mind the relationships between the parts of a sermon. Second, the speaker views his sermon as a whole and thereby heightens his sense of unity. An outline also crystallizes the order of ideas so that the listener will be given them in the appropriate sequence. Finally, the preacher recognizes the places in the outline requiring additional supporting material to develop his points.

Sometimes the arrangement of ideas in the passage will have to be altered in the outline. Because of his readers, the biblical writer may follow an inductive order; but because of his hearers, an expositor may select a deductive plan. Sermons from the epistles fit more easily into outlines than do poems, parables, or narratives. Unless a preacher remains flexible in the ways he communicates passages, he will find it impossible to accomplish the purpose of some passages with his audience. An expositor handling the epilogue of Proverbs, for example, will discover that the passage cannot be outlined logically. Proverbs 31:10–31 consists of a Hebrew acrostic, describing the qualities of a good wife from Aleph to Tau, the *A* to *Z* of the Hebrew alphabet. Although an effective memory device for a Hebrew reader, this acrostic becomes sheer nonsense for English listeners. To teach this passage a preacher must place his own outline upon its subject matter.

Outlines usually consist of an introduction, a body, and a conclusion. Introductions (which will be discussed in greater detail) introduce the subject, the idea, or the first point of the sermon. The body then elaborates on the idea. The conclusion (also to be treated later) brings the idea to a focus and ends the sermon.

Not all points in a sermon have equal importance. Some are more basic than others. The most fundamental become the main points and make up the basic framework around which the sermon is built. These main points stand as Roman numerals in the body of the message. For example:

I. We should praise God because He has elected us in Christ (Eph. 1:4–6).
II. We should praise God because He has dealt with us according to the riches of His grace (1:7–12).
III. We should praise God because He has sealed us with the Holy Spirit until we acquire full possession of our inheritance (1:13–14).

Simply listing these major points, however, does not develop the sermon. Because main points need expansion, secondary points elaborating the main points are added to the outline. A capital letter designates those points and, in addition, they are indented.

I. We should praise God because He has elected us in Christ (Eph. 1:4–6).

    A. He elected us before the foundation of the world (v. 4).

    B. He elected us because He preappointed us to sonship through adoption.

    C. He elected us so that He would be praised for the glory of His grace (v. 6).

The addition of these subpoints improves the outline by making the development clearer and more specific. The outline can be even more complete if it brings in specific details to support the secondary points. Usually an Arabic number and further indentation shows subordination to the main and secondary points. In the sample outline the sermon expands by the addition of detail.

  II. We should praise God because He has dealt with us according to the riches of His grace (1:7–12).

    A. He has remitted our sins through Christ's blood (v. 7).

    B. He has given us wisdom to understand the mystery of His will (vv. 8–10).

      1. His will is according to His good pleasure which He purposed to carry out in Christ (vv. 8–9).

      2. His will purposes to unite all things in Christ at the proper time (v. 10).

With each expansion of the outline, the substance of the sermon becomes more obvious. An individual who had never looked at the passage could read the outline and gain some idea of the speaker's organization and development of the sermon.

If additional development is needed, it is shown by use of small letters and further indentation. A sermon outline, compared to one for a thesis or research paper, should be simple and clear and have relatively few points. A complicated outline broken into several indented subdivisions, while impressing the eye, will only bewilder the audience that must listen to it.

Since each point in the outline represents an idea, it should be a grammatically complete sentence. When words or phrases stand as points, they deceive us because they are incomplete and vague. Partial statements allow thought to slip through our minds like a greased football. While a preacher may carry an abbreviated outline into the pulpit, it will fail him if he uses it in his study.

Each point should be a statement, not a question. Questions do not show relationships because they are not ideas. The points in the outline should answer questions, not raise them. Questions may be used in the delivery of the sermon as transitions introducing new points. Such transitional questions precede a point and are placed in parentheses.

While the preacher sees his outline lying before him on the page, only its contents will be heard by the congregation. They do not hear an outline. This obvious fact makes transitional statements particularly significant since they point up relationships of the parts to the whole. Carefully constructed transitions help the listener to think with the speaker so that together they move through the sermon. An effective transition notifies the audience that the preacher is moving on. It may review where they have been, identify the thought to which they are moving, relate what has been said to the main subject or idea, and interest the hearer in the new thought.

Since clear transitions don't spring readily into the mind, they should be planned in advance. Sometimes both the previous idea and the following idea are stated: "Not only is our worship a divine fellowship, it is also a redeeming fellowship." At other times, if we have stated the previous point explicitly as we completed it, we will omit the review: "But the author tells us something else about our worship; it is a redeeming fellowship." However we do it, transitions state or imply the logical or psychological connection between the introduction and the body, the points within the body, and the body and the conclusion. They answer the question, Why these points in this order? Some transitions accomplish this with a single word or a sentence, but others demand a paragraph to establish the unity, order of points, and movement in the sermon. While they should be written out and included in the outline, transitions will often be amplified and enlarged even more as we actually preach the sermon.

New Concepts

Some forms sermons take:
    idea explained
    proposition proved
    principle applied
    story told
    subject completed
Deductive arrangement
Inductive arrangement
Outline
Transition

Definitions

Deductive arrangement—the idea appears as part of the introduction, and the body explains, proves, or applies it.

Idea explained—the idea is presented in the introduction, and the points of the sermon are steps in the explanation of the idea.

Inductive arrangement—the introduction introduces only the first point in the sermon, then with a strong transition each new point links to the previous point until the idea emerges in the conclusion.

Outline—shows the speaker the relationship between the ideas of the sermon. He can tell at a glance which ideas are superior, subordinate, and coordinate.

Principle applied—the idea is stated in the introduction or first point as a principle of faith or life. The remainder of the sermon applies that principle to daily experience.

Proposition proved—the idea is stated in the introduction like the proposition of a debate. The points are proofs of that proposition.

Story told—a story of Scripture is narrated in such a way that the idea is developed directly or by implication.

Subject completed—the subject of the sermon appears in the

introduction. The main points of the sermon are complements of that subject.

Transition —notifies the audience that the preacher is moving
on by stating (or occasionally by implying) the logical or
psychological connection between the introduction and
the body, the points within the body, and the body and
the conclusion.

Stages in the Development of Expository Messages

1. Selecting the Passage
2. Studying the Passage
3. Discovering the Exegetical Idea
4. Analyzing the Exegetical Idea
5. Formulating the Homiletical Idea
6. Determining the Sermon's Purpose
7. Deciding How to Accomplish This Purpose
8. Outlining the Sermon
9. **Filling in the Sermon Outline,** page 137.

Chapter 7

Making Dry Bones Live

Outlines serve as skeletons of thought, and in most sermons, as in most bodies, the skeleton will not be completely
hidden. We ought not put the outline on vulgar display, however, as if the skeleton were "Exhibit C, Victim of Starvation
in the Holocaust." The most effective means of hiding the
bare bones of a sermon is not by disposing of the skeleton
but by covering it with flesh. Supporting material is to the
outline what skin is to bones or walls to the frame of a house.

Stage 9   Fill in the outline with supporting materials that explain, prove, apply, or amplify the points.

An audience does not respond to abstract ideas, nor has anyone ever been moved to action by reading an outline. If an outline remains undeveloped, therefore, an audience can miss its meaning and remain unconvinced. As the sermon unfolds, listeners raise several questions: "I wonder what he means by that?" "What evidence does he have for that statement?" "Sounds impressive, but how would this work out in life?" To clarify, amplify, prove, or apply his ideas and make them understandable and appealing, a preacher uses a variety of supporting materials.

Restatement

Restatement uses the principle of redundancy to state an idea "in other words." It serves two basic purposes. First, restatement gains clarity. Listeners, unlike readers, must get what is said when we say it. They cannot go back and hear it again. If at first they don't understand us, then we must say it again to make ourselves clear. Clovis G. Chappell employs restatement in his introduction to a sermon on the woman taken in adultery.

> The scholars are uncertain as to where in the sacred record this story belongs. Some think that it does not belong at all. From certain of the ancient manuscripts it is omitted. However, speaking not as a scholar but merely as a Bible reader, I am sure that it does really belong. Here I feel is a true story. If it is not true it is one from which the truth itself might learn. Not only is this story true, but in my judgment it is factual. It is the record of an event that actually took place. It would have taken a superb genius indeed to have invented a story so true to life. Certainly it is consistent with what we know about the scribes and the Pharisees; it is yet more consistent with what we know about Jesus himself.[1]

Restatement impresses the truth on the listener. Say

1. *Questions Jesus Asked* (New York: Abingdon-Cokesbury, 1948; reprint ed., Grand Rapids: Baker, 1974), p. 154.

something once and it can be ignored, but repeat it several times and it will be underlined in his thought and feelings. Advertisers invest millions of dollars to restate their ideas on radio, on television, and in magazines. Peter Marshall emphasizes a point through restatement in his sermon "The Art of Moving Mountains":

> I am sure that each of you has read this statement many times:
> *Prayer Changes Things*
> You have seen it painted on posters which adorn the walls of our Sunday school rooms.
> You have seen it stamped on little metal plates,
> read it in the Bible,
> heard it from the pulpit, oh, so many times.
> But do you believe it?
> Do you actually, honestly, believe that prayer changes things?
> Have you ever had prayer change anything for you?
> Your attitudes
> your circumstances
> your obstacles
> your fears?

Restatement differs from repetition. Repetition says the same thing in the same words; restatement says the same thing in different words. Repetition may profitably be used throughout the sermon like a refrain to reinforce a major idea, but the skillful preacher learns to restate a point several times in different ways.

Explanation and Definition

A definition establishes limits. It sets down what must be included and excluded by a term or statement. Explanation also sets boundaries, but it may do so by amplifying on how ideas relate to one another or what an idea implies. Notice how Earl F. Palmer explains what is meant by the Greek word *erōs*:

Erōs is love that is earned, love that is won from us. It is not
the instinctive love that we have for our parents or our children, our family or our social or racial structure. It is not the
kind of love we have for something like wisdom or mankind.
It is love earned from us because of the compelling excellence
of the person or thing or reality. It is the love of beauty, the
love of power, the love of strength.[2]

Definitions and explanations work in a variety of ways.
We usually define a term or idea by placing it in a broad class
of things of which it is a part. At the same time, however, we
must show how it differs from other things in that class. Classification, therefore, explains both similarities and differences. Palmer says, "*Erōs* is love [the broad class of which it
is a part] that is earned, love that is won from us [how it
differs from other kinds of love]." Sometimes we define and
explain through synonyms. A synonym works, however, only
if it touches a listener's previous experience and makes him
understand and feel the meaning intended. Presumably
everyone knows what cults are; but perhaps they don't know
in the particular way we want, so we may say, "The cults are
the unpaid bills of the church."[3]

Comparison and contrast also develop and explain ideas.
Palmer used both in his explanation of *erōs*.

Preachers also use examples in explanation. Ray C. Sted-
man does this when he asks in a sermon, "What do we mean
when we say a thing is holy?" He answers: "Look at your
Bible and it says, 'Holy Bible.' What makes it holy? The land
of Israel is called, 'The Holy Land' and the city of Jerusalem
is called, 'The Holy City.' Why? There is a quality about all
three which they share in common. They all belong to God.
The Bible is God's book; Israel is God's land; Jerusalem is
God's city—they are God's property! That is why they are
holy; they belong to God."

---

2. *Love Has Its Reasons: An Inquiry into New Testament Love* (Waco, Tex.:
Word, 1977), pp. 38–39.

3. This often-quoted statement appears, for example, in Anthony A. Hoe-
kema, *The Four Major Cults: Christian Science, Jehovah's Witnesses, Mor-
monism, Seventh-Day Adventism* (Grand Rapids: Eerdmans, 1963), p. 1.

Explanation proves difficult if the expositor does not know his audience. The more familiar he is with a subject, the less aware he may be of a congregation's ignorance of it. The people in the pew live in a different intellectual world from their pastor. Indeed they support him financially so that he can study what they cannot. He must not assume that his listeners immediately understand what he is talking about. He owes them a clear explanation of exactly what he means. As a guiding rule, a speaker should define every important term in language the audience understands. Certainly it is better to define too many terms than too few. Explaining the relationships and implications of ideas, we should know the explanation ourselves so clearly that no vagueness exists in our own minds. Then we should work through the steps in the explanation so that they come in a logical or psychological order. A mist in the pulpit becomes a fog in the pew.

Factual Information

Facts consist of observations, examples, statistics, and other data that may be verified apart from the speaker. A preacher makes a factual statement when he declares, "Greek is a rich and varied language having several words for love. But of these words only two, *philia* and *erōs*, exerted much influence in Greek literature or thought in the first century." If a listener cared to do so, he could verify the accuracy of that statement by checking the words the Greeks used for love. In the expository sermon observations about the content of a passage are factual since a hearer can see for himself what the Bible says.

Much that parades as fact is opinion in disguise. "As a matter of fact," a preacher says, "the greatest threat to the morality of America is the television set." Of course that is not a matter of fact at all, only a matter of opinion. That opinion may or may not be valid, depending on the facts. Facts, of course, are stupid things until they are brought into relationship with each other and conclusions are drawn from them. Opinions, on the other hand, are just as stupid unless they are built on facts. The expositor, like any ethical speaker, needs to know his facts and be sure of their validity. "Every man has a right to his own opinion," Bernard Baruch observes, "but no man has a right to be wrong in his facts." Facts not only help the listener understand, they secure respect for the speaker.

Statistics are a special form of facts that enable us to survey a large amount of territory very quickly. They are particularly appealing to citizens in a numbers-conscious society. Indeed the American appetite for statistics seems insatiable, and statisticians crank out an unending supply, ranging from the number of hours an average family watches TV to the percentage of unhappy families in our culture. This allegiance to numbers has created its own pitfalls for the innocent—and opportunities for the dishonest. An air of certainty hangs over the decimal point or the factionalized percentage—even where measurement is unknowable or absurd. A classic illustration is a report made years ago that 33⅓ percent of all coeds at Johns Hopkins University had married faculty members. The percentage was accurate. Johns Hopkins had only three women students at the time, and one of them married a faculty member. Preachers eager to win their point may be particularly susceptible to the unsupported statistic. One noted evangelist reported, "I read not long ago that 50 percent of rock groups practice devil worship and witchcraft, and I believe the figure is rising each day." Who counted? Who was counted? When? Where?

When figures do enter a sermon, they should be as simple as possible without sacrificing accuracy. Round numbers are usually sufficient. While an accountant might be impressed with the information that in 1950 the population of Chicago was 3,620,962, most of us will find the figure "a little over three and a half million" easier to grasp. In working with statistics, data can be made meaningful and vivid by comparing them to things within the experience of the audience.

In describing the temple of Diana in Ephesus we might say, "It was 180 feet wide, over 375 feet long, with columns that towered 60 feet in height," and then add, "That temple was wider and longer than a football field including the end zones, and the columns were taller than a five-story building." A speaker made understandable the small size of an electron by first giving the decimal fraction, which was incomprehensible, and then adding: "If an electron were increased in size till it became as large as an apple, and a human being grew larger in the same proportion, that person could hold the entire solar system in the palm of his hand and would have to use a magnifying glass in order to see it."[4]

Quotations

We introduce quotations to support or expand a point for two reasons: impressiveness and authority. When we discover that someone else has stated the idea more effectively than we can, we use his words. James S. Stewart introduces a sermon on Isaiah 5:30 with a snatch of a phrase from Robert Browning: "Of all the doubts which, as Browning puts it, can 'rap and knock and enter in our soul,' by far the most devastating is doubt of the ultimate purpose of God." Stewart develops his introduction with a series of other quotes, all selected because of the power of their wording. He says:

> ... that is precisely the doubt which is lying like an appalling weight on multitudes of lives to-day. They would think twice before subscribing to Tennyson's faith:
> *Yet I doubt not thro' the ages one increasing purpose runs,*
> *And the thoughts of men are widen'd with the process of*
> *the suns.*
> "Where is any evidence of such a purpose?" they want to ask. ... So they are back where Ecclesiastes was. "Vanity of vanities, all is vanity." What is the use, cried Thomas Hardy, of all your prayers, you praying people, when you have nothing better to pray to than

---

4. Alan H. Monroe, *Principles and Types of Speech*, p. 231.

> *The dreaming, dark, dumb Thing*
> *That turns the handle of this idle Show?*

"A bad joke"—that was Voltaire's final verdict on life. "Ring down the curtain," said the dying actor, "the farce is done."[5]

There are many ways to talk about the place pain plays in our lives. A preacher sums up one perspective by quoting words more impressive than his own: "Pain plants the flag of reality in the fortress of a rebel heart."

Anchoring a point with some wording that digs into the mind is probably the major reason preachers turn to quotations in sermons. When we give credit for the quote, we do so primarily for ethics.

We also include quotations for authority. In this case when we give credit for what we quote, we do so because the person who said it is in a better position to speak than we are. Ernest T. Campbell does this in speaking of times when the seeming futility of what we do causes us to draw back from involvement in social action. Campbell says:

> I was struck the other day by Leonard Woolf's view of his life's work. "I see clearly," he said, "that I have achieved practically nothing. The world today and the history of the human anthill during the past 5-7 years would be exactly the same as it is if I had played ping pong instead of sitting on committees and writing books and memoranda. I have therefore to make a rather ignominious confession that I must have in a long life ground through between 150,000 and 200,000 hours of perfectly useless work."[6]

We also quote others because they are in a better position to know the facts or interpret them or because the audience would be more likely to accept their evaluation. An expositor who knows the Bible and understands people already believes in original sin, but he may quote the report of the Minnesota Crime Commission to a skeptical audience:

---

5. *The Gates of New Life* (New York: Scribner, 1940; reprint ed., Grand Rapids: Baker, 1972), pp. 1–2.

6. *Locked in a Room with Open Doors* (Waco, Tex.: Word, 1974), p. 117.

Every baby starts life as a little savage. He is completely selfish and self-centered. He wants what he wants when he wants it — his bottle, his mother's attention, his playmate's toy, his uncle's watch. Deny him these wants, and he seethes with rage and aggressiveness, which would be murderous, were he not so helpless. He is dirty. He has no morals, no knowledge, no skills. This means that all children, not just certain children, are born delinquent. If permitted to continue in the self-centered world of his infancy, given free reign to his impulsive actions to satisfy his wants, every child would grow up a criminal, a thief, a killer, a rapist.

At other times the expert is better qualified to speak with authority on a subject. D. M. Baillie quotes a historian to demonstrate that early Christians possessed an intellectual quality in their faith:

> Dr. T. R. Glover, who was such an authority on that period [the early centuries A.D.], tells us that one reason why Christianity conquered the world was because it did better thinking than the rest of the world. It not only knew better how to live and how to die: it also knew better how to think. It "out-thought" the world. Here is a deeply interesting passage: "The Christian read the best books, assimilated them, and lived the freest intellectual life the world had. Jesus had set him free to be true to fact. There is no place for an ignorant Christian. From the very start every Christian had to know and to understand, and he had to read the Gospels, he had to be able to give a reason for his faith. They read about Jesus, and they knew him, and they knew where they stood. ... Who did the thinking in that ancient world? Again and again it was the Christian. He out-thought the world."[7]

Authorities must carry credentials. Several questions should be asked about any expert to establish his competence: (1) Does his experience or training qualify him to speak with authority on this subject? (2) Is the testimony based on firsthand knowledge? (3) Is the authority prejudiced? A prejudiced authority does not inspire trust since he will tend to

---

7. *To Whom Shall We Go?* (New York: Scribner, 1955; reprint ed., Grand Rapids: Baker, 1974), pp. 62–63.

look with favor on evidence supporting his opinions and to overlook the rest. A prejudiced authority speaking against his bias can of course make an excellent witness. George Bernard Shaw speaking on behalf of Christianity would be strong support since he often spoke out against it. (4) How does the audience regard his testimony? Do they know him? Do they respect him? When an obscure individual is used as an authority, we should tell the audience his qualifications to speak to the issue.[8]

Quotes should be used sparingly in a sermon. A message from the pulpit ought not sound like a term paper. Generally quotes should be brief. Long quotations often become unclear and hinder communication. Sometimes a longer quote may be paraphrased and then a few important sentences from the quotation read directly to the audience.

Quotations will be enhanced if we introduce them into the sermon with a touch of freshness. It requires little effort to draw in a quote with "Spurgeon said," "Paul wrote," or "the Bible says." More thought is demanded but more accomplished if we rearrange them: "Written boldly into the Bible is this phrase ..." "Paul felt keenly that ..." "This is what Charles Dickens was trying to tell us when he observed ..." "You can see then the significance of those words embedded in verse 10 ..."

Narration

When we gossip, we gossip not about ideas but about people. When popular newsmagazines such as *Time* handle compound-complex subjects such as the economy or political upheaval in China, they do so in part by discussing the people involved. Narration within a sermon describes the individuals and events embraced in biblical accounts. Every passage has its people—sometimes they stand there laugh-

8. Monroe, *Principles and Types of Speech*, p. 233.

ing, cursing, praying, and at other times they hide and we must look for them. In every text, though, there is always somebody writing and somebody reading. Pull aside a doctrine and you'll find personalities. For example, grace does not exist in cold storage in heaven. There is only someone giving grace and another receiving it. The Holy Spirit knew the value of narration when He filled the Scriptures with it, and Jesus demonstrated the impact of narration in the parables He told.

Narration can supply background in a sermon by filling in the history, setting, or personalities involved. John Hercus uses it effectively to make us live with David as he wrote Psalm 24:

> David sat up straight, stretched his arms and yawned. It had been a day of rehearsing, going over the whole processional routine with the musicians, the singers, and the ballet. The score and the choreography were well advanced, and David was more than satisfied. The psalm was good—short, clear, well-suited to the occasion. Hm-m-m-m-m ... that was a choice phrase about "ascend the hill of the Lord ... stand in His holy place." Very good. It would make a fine background for work with the cymbals and trumpets and chorus. And the ballet would have splendid chances, under his leadership, to express their rising feeling of spiritual drama.
>
> And those four conditions of entry into the holy place— they were just right. Terse, compact, neat. Clean hands, pure heart, no accent on trashy values (that's really what he meant by "does not lift up his soul to what is false") and no cheating or being deceitful. Yes, indeed, that checks a man out as fully and completely as you could wish.
>
> Clean hands ... like his own clean hands ...
>
> Suddenly a memory flashed into his mind. A memory of washing, washing, washing those "clean" hands of his, trying to scrub away a bloody thing that could not be undone. How did it happen? Oh yes ... because of Michal.[9]

Narration takes on energy when the verbs and nouns paint pictures on our minds. Sometimes a different view-

---

9. *David*, 2d ed. (Chicago: Inter-Varsity, 1968), pp. 55–56.

point brings freshness to an oft-told account. How did the woman taken in adultery or the woman at the well think of Jesus when they first met Him? In the epistles Paul pictures an objector jumping up to argue with him: "What advantage . . . is there in being a Jew?" (Rom. 3:1 NIV), someone asks. "Food for the stomach and the stomach for food" (I Cor. 6:12 NIV), argues a hedonist of the time. What were they like? Can you describe how they might have carried on the discussion?

Use dialogue. The Gospel narratives and the parables are filled with it. Put words into people's mouths. When only one person appears, use soliloquy or "self-talk." That's what Hercus did with David, and it's what Jesus did with the shrewd branch manager (Luke 16:2–7) and the destitute boy in the far country (Luke 15:11–32). The lad asks himself, "How many hired servants of my father's have bread enough and to spare, and I perish here with hunger!" (v. 17 ASV).

Narration means communicating with imagination, and imagination reflects the insights of faith. Imagination is half brother to interpretation since both relate to the text. We determine what a passage means from what a passage says. So imagination goes one step beyond the biblical facts and yet stays tied to them.

Illustrations

S. I. Hayakawa's advice for speakers wanting to develop clarity is to study a cookbook since recipes explain general concepts by breaking them down to their specifics. For example, a recipe for Beef Wellington reads: "Place tenderloin on rack in open roasting pan. Do not add water. Do not cover. Roast in a 425° oven, 20 to 25 minutes." Hayakawa's counsel is particularly helpful for specialists, whose extensive knowledge of a subject can keep them from being effective communicators. Their education moves them away from particulars to the vague realms of abstraction.

A theologian for example speaks about *harmartiology*

instead of *sin* because the abstract word serves as a better umbrella for the varied aspects of the topic. When the theologian addresses an audience less familiar with his discipline, though, he must step down from his abstraction and talk about murder, lying, stealing, or adultery. If he cannot or will not do this, though he may get high marks as a scholar, he fails as a communicator. Sören Kierkegaard complained that when he asked the philosopher Georg Hegel for directions to a street address in Copenhagen, all he received was the map of Europe.

Skilled preachers deal in high and low levels of abstraction, climbing back and forth like a laborer on a ladder. To have meaning, particulars must be gathered up in generalizations, and abstractions must be taken down to particulars to be made understandable. "The interesting writer, the informative speaker, the accurate thinker, and the sane individual, operate on all levels of the abstraction ladder, moving quickly and gracefully in orderly fashion from higher to lower, from lower to higher — with minds as lithe and deft and beautiful as monkeys in a tree."[10]

One means of earthing our sermons lies in the use of illustrations. Well-chosen, skillfully used illustrations restate, explain, validate, or apply ideas by relating them to tangible experiences. To nail a truth into the mind requires that we hit it several times. While most restatement comes through the repetition of propositional statements, illustrations can present the truth still another time without wearying the listeners. Understanding too may be gained through analogies and anecdotes. An illustration, like the picture on television, makes clear what the speaker explains.

Illustrations also render truth believable. Logically, of course, examples cannot stand as proof, but psychologically they work with argument to gain acceptance. A preacher arguing that all truth is equally valid but not equally valuable may use an analogy to get his audience to accept what he

---

10. S. I. Hayakawa, *Language in Thought and Action*, p. 190.

says. A penny and a dollar bill are both genuine, he may point out, but they are not of equal worth. Therefore we must distinguish between penny- and dollar-truth. The analogy wins as much agreement as the reasoned argument.

Illustrations apply ideas to experience. A listener needs not only to understand and accept a concept but also to know what difference it makes. Examples display truth in action. William E. Sangster preached a sermon based on Genesis 41:51 developing the idea, "We must remember to forget." He concludes his sermon with an anecdote:

> It was Christmas time in my home. One of my guests had come a couple of days early and saw me sending off the last of my Christmas cards. He was startled to see a certain name and address. "Surely, you are not sending a greeting card to him," he said.
>
> "Why not?" I asked.
>
> "But you remember," he began, "eighteen months ago . . ."
>
> I remembered, then, the thing the man had publicly said about me, but I remembered also resolving at the time with God's help, that I had remembered to forget. And God had "made" me forget!
>
> I posted the card.

Illustrations serve a preacher and his congregation in other ways. They aid memory, stir emotion, create need, hold attention, and establish rapport between speaker and hearer.[11]

The foundational principle for the use of illustrations is that illustrations should illustrate. According to its etymology *to illustrate* means "to throw light on a subject." Therefore there is no such thing as "a good illustration" but only a good illustration of a particular truth. Illustrations resemble a row of footlights illuminating the action on a stage. If a footlight shines in the eyes of the audience, it blinds them to

---

11. Ian Macpherson lists seventeen purposes served by illustrations in *The Art of Illustrating Sermons*, pp. 13–33.

what they ought to see.[12] A story told for its own sake may entertain or amuse, but it gets in the way of the sermon. An anecdote works in the service of truth only when it centers attention on the idea and not on itself.

Illustrations should also be understandable. Through examples we clarify the unknown with the known. If the illustration needs to be explained to make it clear, it should not be used. To explain an illustration, which in turn explains a concept, is to clarify the unfamiliar with the unfamiliar. Examples taken from the Bible sometimes violate this rule by illustrating the unknown with the unknown. In a day of biblical illiterates, biblical stories may be as remote to modern listeners as Chinese history. Using them as illustrations of other biblical passages can be an exercise in futility. If stories from the Bible are told, the expositor must take time and care to relate them so that an audience enters into them and feels their force. Because a communicator illumines the unknown through the known, the most effective illustrations touch as close to the lives of the listeners as possible. Among the most effective are "human interest" stories, which deal with subjects of our common life such as children, animals, and comic strips.

Illustrations should be convincing. As much as lies in him, the preacher should be sure of his facts. While a factually inaccurate story might clearly illustrate an idea, the preacher who uses it with an audience aware of its inaccuracy will undermine his credibility. What is more, illustrations ought not offend the good sense of an audience. Truth may be stranger than fiction, but improbable anecdotes only lead the audience to suspect that the preacher is strange. If an incident sounds far-fetched, acknowledge that and then give support for it.

Ministers seem to beget children who talk in illustrations. When too many such stories punctuate sermons, skeptical congregations cannot help but wonder whether the preacher

---

12. John Nicholls Booth, *The Quest for Preaching Power*, p. 146.

always speaks truth. Because personal illustrations carry force, preachers fall to the temptation of relating stories as though they happened to them when in reality they did not. The gospel sits in judgment on the methods used to proclaim it, and God's truth cannot be benefited by our falsehoods. Should a congregation suspect that we will lie to make a point, they have reason to believe that we will lie to make a convert.

Illustrations should be appropriate to the theme of the sermon and to the audience. Great themes may be hurt by their illustrations. One preacher eager to emphasize the omnipresence of God declared, "God is even in the trash can!" What the illustration held in accuracy, it lacked in appropriateness. Some illustrations acceptable to one audience might not be appropriate for another. For example, this story, while reflecting on the morality of our age, would have to be weighed for its appropriateness with different groups: A man sat in a restaurant chatting with an attractive young woman. In the course of the conversation, he pointed to a well-dressed young man seated at a corner table.

"See that fellow over there? If he offered you $500 to go to bed with him tonight, would you do it?"

"Five hundred dollars?" the girl responded. "Well, for $500 I guess I would."

A few minutes later the man pointed to another fellow seated at another part of the room.

"See that guy? Suppose he offered you $20 to spend the night with him. Would you do it?"

"Twenty dollars?" the girl sniffed. "Of course not. What do you think I am?"

The man replied, "Oh, I've already found that out. I'm just trying to establish your price!"

That illustration might be perfectly acceptable on a college campus or in a talk to businessmen, but a minister would have to consider carefully whether or not it were appropriate for his Sunday-morning congregation.

Illustrations should be told dramatically. A sculptor was

asked how he carved a statue of a lion when he didn't have a model. He explained, "I simply carved away anything that didn't look like a lion." That is good advice for preachers too. A skillful storyteller cuts away surplus details that fail to contribute to the punch line of his story. Narrative illustrations should use dialogue and direct quotation so that the preacher relives the story rather than merely retells it. The story should be told as dramatically as possible so that the audience enters into the illustration and feels, as well as understands, the point being made.

Good illustrations can be found everywhere. Personal experience is a particularly prolific source. Every life is a circus, but some people can gather more material in a stroll around the neighborhood than others can find in a trip around the world. The difference lies not in what we experience, but in what we see in our experiences. We must observe in order to see. The world can be God's picture book if we see in ordinary events of life analogies and applications of spiritual truth.

Personal illustrations add warmth and vitality to a sermon, but three general rules should govern their use. First, the illustration should be true. It should also be modest. Congregations dislike first-person stories when the preacher emerges regularly as the hero. We react negatively to a conversationalist who brags about how clever, humorous, or spiritual he is. Nothing changes that reaction when the boasting is done from the pulpit. Most experiences of course make us neither victors nor villains and can be recounted with modesty and great benefit. If a personal illustration is used, it should be told without apology. When a preacher says, "If you will pardon the personal illustration," he directs attention to what should not be noticed. If the incident should be used, then there is no need to apologize. If it should not be used, an apology will not help. A third rule that must be scrupulously observed in using personal experiences is that we must not violate a confidence. People resent sharing a concern with their pastor and wondering if they will appear as part of his sermon. Even when some personal incident can be shared without anyone being hurt, ask permission to use it. Even though *you* may feel you are flattering people, *they* may resent the public exposure.

Illustrations also come from reading. Few ministers can afford to read without pen in hand for recording materials that will illuminate their sermons. Comic strips, nursery rhymes, magazines, newspapers, novels, history all provide source material for messages. Sermons by gifted preachers provide illustrations in context that makes them superior to collections where stories usually appear divorced from what they illustrate.

Certainly many illustrations will come to the preacher as he works on a sermon. Let him write down clearly the point to be made and then let him think of the relationships within that point demanding illumination. Often his mind and memory will supply what he needs. The ability to fashion appropriate analogies or to come up with apt applications can be developed through practice.

Undoubtedly the place to which a preacher turns most often for supporting material is his file. What he gets out of his file for a given sermon depends completely on what he has put into it. Many systems have been developed to enable a minister to save the results of his study and reading. Usually two kinds of files must be kept. One, the letter-sized file, stores sermon notes, large sheets of paper, booklets, or even pages torn from unwanted books. This file may be broken down according to subjects and books of the Bible. The Dewey decimal system, used by most libraries, can form the basis of the subject file. The Rossin-Dewey subject list relates the Dewey system to a pastor's special needs.[13] Another simple and efficient system designed for ministers is the *New Baker's Textual and Topical Filing System.*[14]

In addition to a large, letter-sized file, a minister should

---

13. Available from the Shepherd Company, Hopkins, MN 55343.

14. Grand Rapids: Baker, 1976.

also develop a smaller 3- by 5-inch card file. One section of
this file may be divided into the books of the Bible, with the
cards arranged under each book according to chapter and
verse. Here illustrations, exegetical notes, bibliography per-
taining to particular passages of the Scripture are stored. Another section of the card file should be indexed according to
subjects. This file may be broken down by the first letter and
first vowel in the subject. The system is set up in the following manner:

Aa	Ae	Ai	Ao	Au
Ba	Be	Bi	Bo	Bu
Ca	Ce	Ci	Co	Cu
Da	De	Di	Do	Du
Ea	Ee	Ei	Eo	Eu
etc.				

Illustrations of the subject "love" would be filed under
Lo (*L* is the first letter, and *o* the first vowel); "example"
under *Ea*; or "atonement" under *Ao*. The advantage of this
system lies in its simplicity and versatility. Most material that
should be kept as supporting material in a sermon—anecdotes, quotes, poems, exegetical notes, analogies, bibliographic references—can be filed on 3 × 5 cards.

A minister needs a filing system. Any system that allows
him to store information is superior to no system at all. The
filing system also needs the minister. No system will work
unless he determines to work it. Agur, a writer of Proverbs,
commends the ant for its great wisdom: "The ants—they are
no strong folk, yet they lay up their food in the summer"
(Prov. 30:25). Wise is the preacher who learns a lesson from
the ant.

Stage
Nine

155

New Concepts

Repetition
Restatement
Explanation
Definition
Factual information
Quotations
Narration
Illustrations

Definitions

Definition —establishes what must be included and excluded
by a term or statement.
Explanation —sets boundaries by amplifying on how ideas
relate to one another or what an idea implies.
Factual information —consists of observations, examples,
statistics, and other data that may be verified apart from
the preacher.

Narration —describes who did what to whom with what effect in the biblical accounts. It can be used to supply
background in a sermon by discussing the history, setting, or personalities involved in a passage.
Illustrations —restate, explain, prove, or apply ideas by relating them to tangible experiences.

Stages in the Development
of Expository Messages

1. Selecting the Passage
2. Studying the Passage
3. Discovering the Exegetical Idea
4. Analyzing the Exegetical Idea
5. Formulating the Homiletical Idea
6. Determining the Sermon's Purpose
7. Deciding How to Accomplish This Purpose
8. Outlining the Sermon
9. Filling in the Sermon Outline
10. **Preparing the Introduction and Conclusion,** page 159.

Chapter 8

Start with a Bang and Quit All Over

Introductions and conclusions have significance in a sermon out of proportion to their length. During the introduction an audience gains impressions of a speaker that often determine whether or not they will accept what he says. If he appears nervous, hostile, or unprepared, they are inclined to reject him. If he seems alert, friendly, and interesting, they decide he is an able person with a positive attitude toward himself and his listeners.

159

Stage 10   Prepare the introduction and conclusion of the sermon.

The Introduction

An introduction introduces the congregation to the idea and its development. The characteristics of effective introductions will grow out of that purpose.

Commands Attention

An introduction should command attention. When a minister steps behind the pulpit, he dare not assume that his congregation sits expectantly on the edge of the pews waiting for his sermon. In reality they are probably a bit bored and harbor a suspicion that he will make matters worse. A Russian proverb offers wise counsel to the preacher: "It is the same with men as with donkeys: whoever would hold them fast must get a very good grip on their ears!" The opening words of a sermon therefore need not be dramatic; they need not even be plain; but they must go after the minds of the hearers to force them to listen. If the preacher does not capture attention in the first thirty seconds, he may never gain it at all.

The possibilities for an opening statement that demands attention are as wide as a minister's creativity. He may start with a paradox: "Many children of God live as though they were orphans."

He may use a familiar thought in an unfamiliar setting: " 'Honesty is the best policy.' When a person says that, he may not be honest at all. He may simply be shrewd."

Rhetorical questions reach for attention: "If it were possible for God to die and He died this morning, how long would it take you to find out?"

A startling fact or statistic gets an audience to listen: "One out of three marriages ends in the divorce court. Only one marriage in six is happy."

Having read his text, the preacher can make a provocative comment about it: "There is a delicious touch of humor about this text. Jesus is deadly serious, but that fact does not interfere with his laughter."[1]

At times humor wins attention: "A businessman, completing his annual checkup, was assured by his physician, 'Sir, you're as sound as a dollar!' The man fainted."

The passage itself can be the basis of attention: "For many people Hebrews chapter six is the most perplexing passage in the Bible." The expositor may go directly to the passage: "This morning I'd like to begin by making a confession. I'd like to bring you the message of another preacher. That is, after all, the way Solomon, the author of Ecclesiastes, introduces himself."

People sit up and listen at the prospect of a story: "Mary Watson was a housewife in her late thirties. She thought of herself as young and still attractive even though she had been married fifteen years and was the mother of three children. In the space of a month she developed into an ugly, old woman."

At other times the preacher will drive directly to his subject: "If you claim to be a Christian, you must believe in the Trinity."

However he begins, the minister should make the most of his first twenty-five words to seize attention. An ear-grabbing opening promises that what follows may be worth thirty minutes of everyone's time.

Surfaces Needs

An effective introduction also surfaces need. A preacher must turn involuntary attention into voluntary attention, so that people listen not only because they ought to but because they want to. Paul O'Neil, a writer for *Life* magazine, evolved O'Neil's Law: "Always grab the reader by the throat in the

1. Clovis G. Chappell, *Questions Jesus Asked* (Nashville: Abingdon, 1948; reprint ed., Grand Rapids: Baker, 1974), p. 30.

first paragraph, sink your thumbs into his windpipe in the second and hold him against the wall until the tag line."[2] Social scientist Arthur R. Cohen concluded that when audiences receive information that meets felt needs, two things happen: (1) more learning takes place; and (2) opinions change faster and more permanently than when information is given and then not applied to life.[3] All of this says that the important point of contact with a congregation lies in answering, "Why bring this up? Why do I need to listen?"

Charles R. Swindoll began a sermon on II Corinthians 1:3–11 by raising a question that exposes the raw nerve of need:

> El Tablazo looked so close. Too close. It happened so fast. Exploding into the jagged 14,00v-foot peak, the DC-4 disintegrated with a metallic scream.
>
> What was left of the Avianca Airline flight bound for Quito, Ecuador, flamed crazily down the mountainside into a deep ravine. One awful moment illuminated a cold Colombian mountain in the night, then the darkness returned. And the silence.
>
> Before leaving the airport earlier that day, a young New Yorker named Glenn Chambers hurriedly scribbled a note on a piece of paper he found on the floor of the terminal. The scrap was part of a printed advertisement with a single word, "Why?" sprawled across the center.
>
> Needing stationery in a hurry, Chambers scrawled a note to his mother around the word in the middle. Quickly folding this last-minute thought, he stuffed it in an envelope and dropped it in a box. There would be more to come, of course. More about the budding of a lifelong dream to begin a ministry with the *Voice of the Andes* in Ecuador.
>
> But there was no more to come. Between the mailing and the delivery of Chambers' note, El Tablazo snagged his flight and his dreams from the night sky. The envelope arrived later

---

2. In George P. Hunt, "Editor's Note: Attila the Hun in a Tattered Sweater," *Life*, 13 November 1964, p. 3.

3. "Need for Cognition and Order of Communication as Determinants of Opinion Change," in *The Order of Presentation in Persuasion*, by Carl I. Hovland et al. (New Haven, Conn.: Yale University, 1957), pp. 79–97.

than the news of his death. When his mother received it, the question burned up at her from the page—Why?

It is the question that hits first and lingers longest. Why? Why me? Why now? Why this?[4]

Need can be touched quickly. Asking "Can a woman who works be a good mother? What do you say? What does the Bible say?" touches need in less than twenty words.

Sermons catch fire when flint strikes steel. When the flint of a person's problem strikes the steel of the Word of God, a spark ignites that burns in the mind. Directing our preaching at people's needs is not a mere persuasive technique; it is the task of the ministry. Leslie J. Tizard understood what preaching must be about when he declared, "Whoever will become a preacher must feel the needs of men until it becomes an obsession of his soul."[5]

Needs take many shapes and forms. Believers differ from unbelievers not in their needs but in the ways their needs are met. Abraham H. Maslow, a noted psychologist, believes that needs build on one another. Throughout our lives we move from one cluster of needs to another as motivations for our actions.[6] One basic set of needs, he argues, springs from our bodies. These physiological needs are met by food, drink, recreation, sexual expression, and elimination, and if they are not met, they dominate thought and life.

Men and women have needs that result from living with other people. Social-dependency needs include the desire for esteem, love and affection, security, self-realization and self-expression. People want to know that they are loved, that they have worth, that they can grow, develop, and realize their potential.

People also need to know and understand. Maslow maintains that curiosity as a strong motivation comes only after

---

4. *For Those Who Hurt* (Portland: Multnomah, 1977).

5. *Preaching: The Art of Communication*.

6. *Motivation and Personality*, 2d ed. (New York: Harper & Row, 1970).

physical and social-dependency needs have been met. Curiosity may catch attention at the beginning of a sermon. But it will not cause people to respond at the same depth as when they understand how God meets their longing for self-esteem, security, affection, and love.

Early in the sermon, therefore, listeners should realize that the pastor is talking to them about them. He raises a question, probes a problem, identifies a need, opens up a vital issue to which the passage speaks. Application starts in the introduction, not in the conclusion. Should a preacher of even limited ability bring to the surface people's questions, problems, hurts, and desires to deal with them from the Bible, he will be acclaimed a genius. More important than that, he will through his preaching bring the grace of God to bear on the agonizing worries and tensions of daily life.

Introduces Body of Sermon

Introductions should orient the congregation to the body of the sermon and its development. An introduction should introduce. At the very least it should introduce the sermon's subject so that no one need guess what the preacher plans to talk about. If the subject alone is introduced, then the major points usually complete it. For example, if the minister raises the question "How can we know the will of God?," the audience expects the major assertions of the body to provide the answer.

The introduction may go beyond the subject and orient hearers to the main idea. An exposition of Romans 1:1–17 that raises the issue of what must be done to evangelize society may lead to the statement, "When the effect of the gospel is all-important in the church, the force of the gospel is unstoppable in the world." Once the idea has been stated, however, the preacher must then raise one of these basic questions about it: What does this mean? Is it true? What difference does it make? While he may not use these words, he should bring up one of these questions. If he fails to do so, directly or indirectly, the sermon is over even though he speaks for another thirty minutes. Effective sermons maintain a sense of tension—the feeling that something more must be said if the message is to be complete. When the tension goes, the sermon ends. Therefore, through the developmental questions the preacher explores what must be done with the idea in the remainder of the sermon. It may develop as an idea explained, a proposition proved, or a principle applied.

In sermons developed inductively, the introduction leads into the first main point. As far as the audience knows, the first point could be the entire message. The first point must then be linked to the second point by a strong transition, and in the same way the second to the third, until the complete idea of the sermon emerges.

Exhibits Other Characteristics

Other things may be said about introductions. A sermon should not be opened with an apology. Through an apology the speaker hopes to win sympathy; at best he gains pity. A congregation will not be persuaded by that preacher. If you are unprepared, let the congregation discover it for themselves. In many cases they will never find out.

Keep the introduction short. After you get water, stop pumping. Unfortunately no percentages help us here. An introduction needs to be long enough to capture attention, raise needs, and orient the audience to the subject, the idea, or the first point. Until that is done, the introduction is incomplete; after that the introduction is too long. An old woman said of the Welsh preacher John Owen that he was so long spreading the table, she lost her appetite for the meal.

An introduction should not promise more than it delivers. When it does, it is like firing off a cannon to shoot out a pea. Sensational introductions to mediocre sermons resemble broken promises. When the preacher fails to meet the need he has raised, the congregation feels cheated.

Some place at the opening of the sermon, the preacher should read the Scriptures. Some men place the Scripture reading immediately before the sermon since the sermon should be an exposition of the passage. Unfortunately, unless the text is read skillfully, congregations may regard it as a necessary boredom that comes before they settle down to hear what is said about the Bible. As a general rule, short passages should come after the introduction. When the Scripture follows the introduction, the audience has a mindset that helps them pay attention to the reading.

Use humor carefully. If it directs attention to the idea, laughter serves as a splendid tool. When it merely entertains, humor makes the sermon seem like a letdown. In facing a new audience humor helps a speaker build a bridge, but too many jokes may cause them to write him off as a comedian. When humor is used, therefore, it should relate the audience to the minister or his message.

How a minister steps into the pulpit tells the audience a lot about him. If he moves in an unhurried, confident manner, his body language communicates that he has something important to say and that the audience would do well to listen. Before he speaks, the preacher should pause to capture attention. He and the congregation ought to start together even though they might not finish together. He should look at the people, not at his notes or even at his Bible.

Nervousness occasionally makes the voice high and squeaky. Therefore a preacher needs control in order to speak his opening words in a composed, relaxed manner. Running the tongue to the back of the mouth or yawning with the mouth shut, which can be done while waiting to speak, reduces tension in the throat. A deep breath before starting also puts a speaker at ease. A large, definite gesture after the first sentences can direct nervous energy into positive bodily movement. Most of all, nervousness and tension will be reduced if the minister knows before he gets to his feet exactly how he will begin his sermon.

There are three types of preachers: those to whom you cannot listen; those to whom you can listen; and those to whom you must listen. During the introduction the congregation usually decides the kind of speaker addressing them that morning.

The Conclusion

As an experienced pilot knows that landing an airplane demands special concentration, so an able preacher understands that conclusions require thoughtful preparation. Like the pilot a skilled preacher should never have uncertainty about where his sermon will land.

In fact the conclusion possesses such importance that many craftsmen prepare it first so that the sermon will proceed toward it in a direct path. Whether or not a minister uses that technique, he must work on his conclusion with special care. Otherwise everything comes to nothing.

The purpose of the conclusion is to conclude—not merely to stop. It should be more than a swipe at getting out of an awkward situation: "May God help us live in the light of these great truths." It should be more than asking the congregation to bow in prayer so that the preacher can sneak off when they're not looking. He should conclude, and the sermon should produce a feeling of finality. Like a lawyer, a minister asks for a verdict. The congregation should see the idea entire and complete, and listeners should know and feel what God's truth demands of them. Directly or indirectly the conclusion answers the question, So what? What difference does this make? And the people face another question: Am I willing to allow God to make that difference in my experience? Paul Whiteman understood the demands of introductions and conclusions when he advised, "When you begin, start with a bang, and when you quit, quit all over!"

Conclusions take different shapes and forms, depending on the sermon, the audience, and the minister. Since the element of freshness adds interest to preaching, a minister will work to vary his conclusions. What are some elements used to land a sermon?

A Summary

In many conclusions a preacher looks back over the terrain and restates points covered along the way. In doing this, however, he reviews the important assertions in order to bind them into the major idea of the sermon. A summary ties loose ends together. It should not be a second preaching of the sermon.

An Illustration

An anecdote summarizing the idea or showing how it works out in life adds impact to a conclusion. The illustration must be exactly on target so that listeners grasp the meaning in a flash without explanation. Having offered the illustration, stop. Make the illustration so transparent that only a sentence or two needs to be added—and even more power comes when it does not need even those.

Peter Marshall ends a sermon on James 4:14 with this gripping story:

> An old legend tells of a merchant in Bagdad who one day sent his servant to the market. Before very long the servant came back, white and trembling, and in great agitation said to his master: "Down in the market place I was jostled by a woman in the crowd, and when I turned around I saw it was Death that jostled me. She looked at me and made a threatening gesture. Master, please lend me your horse, for I must hasten away to avoid her. I will ride to Samarra and there I will hide, and Death will not find me."
>
> The merchant lent him his horse and the servant galloped away in great haste. Later the merchant went down to the market place and saw Death standing in the crowd. He went over to her and asked, "Why did you frighten my servant this morning? Why did you make a threatening gesture?"

"That was not a threatening gesture," Death said. "It was only a start of surprise. I was astonished to see him in Bagdad, for I have an appointment with him tonight in Samarra."

Each of us has an appointment in Samarra. But that is cause for rejoicing—not for fear, provided we have put our trust in Him who alone holds the keys of life and death.[7]

A Quotation

A well-chosen quote used in the conclusion sometimes states the sermon idea in words stronger and more vivid than the preacher can find himself. A quotation should be short, and the preacher should have it memorized. A few lines taken from a poem or a hymn may capture truth dramatically. Generally poetry should be brief, as well as clear and to the point. When a hymn quoted is then sung by the congregation, its impact may be doubled. Again a single sentence taken from the Scripture expounded may sum up the entire passage or apply it. When that verse is quoted again, its force, strengthened by the sermon, can nail the truth to a listener's mind.

A Question

An appropriate question or even a series of questions can conclude a sermon effectively. A sermon on the good Samaritan ended: "Let me conclude where I began. Do you love God? That's splendid. I'm glad to hear that. But do you love your neighbor? How can we talk about loving God whom we have not seen when we do not love our brothers and our neighbors whom we do see?"

A Prayer

A prayer makes a fitting conclusion only when it is an honest petition and not a device to summarize the sermon or

7. *John Doe, Disciple: Sermons for the Young in Spirit*, ed. Catherine Marshall (New York: McGraw-Hill, 1963), pp. 219–20.

make an indirect application to the audience. When a desire for God's work emerges from a response to the sermon, then it can be expressed in an earnest prayer.

Specific Directions

A bit of doggerel reports that:

> *As Tommy Snooks and Bessie Brooks*
> *Were walking out on Sunday,*
> *Said Tommy Snooks to Bessie Brooks,*
> *Tomorrow will be Monday.*

While this might be nominated as the ultimate low in social conversation, for a preacher it ranks high. What can people do to act on the Sunday sermon in Monday morning's world? A conclusion can answer that; and if the preacher does not face this question with his congregation, they may not be able to answer it at all. Not every sermon can end with "how to do it." Some preaching explores great questions, and it accomplishes its purpose when people understand the problem and its biblical solution. No clear, specific duty can be spelled out. Yet preaching comes closer to being incorporated into the structures of life when the minister offers practical guidance on how to translate truth into experience.

Visualization

In the mountain passes of the Pacific Northwest, highway signs warn motorists, "Beware of Falling Rock." Unfortunately when those massive boulders tumble from their resting places, it is usually too late to dodge them. Not all truth can be acted on immediately. Much preaching prepares people for the rocks that may crash in upon them unexpectedly in some indefinite future. Visualization projects a congregation into the future and pictures a future situation in which they might apply what they have learned. Visualization must be probable enough so that anyone can imagine himself in the situation before it takes place. In closing a sermon, a preacher might visualize: "I do not know when it may happen to you or how. Some dark night you may be awakened from a deep sleep by the insistent jangle of your telephone. You will reach over to answer it only to hear a voice on the other end say, 'Prepare yourself for a shock—I have some terrible news.' At that moment you may see the things you've given your life to broken, or someone with whom you have linked your life taken. As life crumbles in about you, you will need to take hold on this unshakable truth. God is too kind ever to be cruel and too wise ever to make a mistake."[8]

Some general observations need to be made about conclusions, whatever form they take. New material should not be introduced in a conclusion. These final moments should drive home what has been said, and they must not take the audience off into new avenues of thought. The sermon itself moves the guns into position; now is the time to fire the shot at the listener's mind and emotions.

If we pretend to be honest, we must not tell our congregations that we intend to conclude and then fail to do so. Words such as "finally" or "in conclusion" too often promise what they don't deliver. In fact words such as those should be used sparingly. In a well-planned sermon, conclusions should conclude without announcing their appearance.

Conclusions need not be long. At times a sudden stop can have penetrating effect. Poorly prepared conclusions that wander about looking for an exit line leave the congregation looking toward the exit. In the words of an old farmer, "When you're through the pumpin', let go the handle." William E. Sangster puts it clearly:

---

8. For an extended discussion of visualization, see Alan H. Monroe, *Principles and Types of Speech*, pp. 327–29.

Having come to the end, stop. Do not cruise about looking for a spot to land, like some weary swimmer coming in from the sea and splashing about until he can find a shelving beach up which to walk. Come right in, and land at once. Finish what you have to say and end at the same time. If the last phrase can have some quality of crisp memorableness, all the better, but do not grope even for that. Let your sermon have the quality that Charles Wesley coveted for his whole life: let the work and the course end together.[9]

9. *The Craft of Sermon Construction*, p. 150.

New Concepts

Introduction
Major characteristics of an effective introduction
Conclusion

Definitions

Conclusion — gives the congregation a view of the idea, entire and complete, and drives home its truth to the mind and life.

Introduction — exposes the congregation to the subject, major idea, or first point of the sermon.

Major characteristics of an effective introduction — commands attention for the idea, raises need, orients the congregation to the body of the sermon and its development.

173

Chapter 9

The Dress of Thought

The preacher of Ecclesiastes waits until the conclusion to write down his credentials: "Not only was the Teacher wise," he says with unsettling candor, "but also he imparted knowledge to the people. He pondered and searched out and set in order many proverbs. The Teacher searched to find just the right words, and what he wrote was upright and true" (Eccles. 12:9–10 NIV). To impart knowledge and to search and find the right words, the ancient preacher wrote a manuscript.

Not all preachers write out sermons, nor do preachers who write out sermons write every sermon, but the discipline of preparing a manuscript improves preaching. Writing scrapes the fungus off thought, arranges ideas in order, and underlines the important ideas. "Writing," to quote Francis Bacon, "makes an exact man exact in thought and in speech."

Of all people an expository preacher professing a high view of inspiration should respect language. To affirm that the individual words of Scripture must be God-breathed and then to ignore his own choice of language smacks of gross inconsistency. His theology, if not his common sense, should tell him that ideas and words cannot be separated. Like jello, concepts assume the mold of the words into which they are poured. As pigments define the artist's concept, so words capture and color the preacher's thought.

The wise man of Proverbs compares the word fitly spoken to "apples of gold in baskets of silver" (25:11). "The difference between the right word and almost the right word," wrote Mark Twain, "is the difference between lightning and lightning bug." Like any skillful author, English poet John Keats understood how style shapes ideas. One evening as he sat in his study with his friend Leigh Hunt, Hunt read while Keats labored over a poem. At one point Keats glanced up and asked, "Hunt, what do you think of this? 'A beautiful thing is an unending joy.' "

"Good," said Hunt, "but not quite perfect."

There was silence for a while, then Keats looked up again. "How about this? 'A thing of beauty is an unending joy.' "

"Better," replied his friend, "but still not quite right."

Keats once more bent over his desk, his pen making quiet scratching noises on the paper. Finally he asked, "Now what do you think of this? 'A thing of beauty is a joy forever.' "

"That," said Hunt, "will live as long as the English language is spoken!"

Who could underestimate the power of words? Most of the Scriptures we love best are those that express truth in delightful language—Psalm 23, I Corinthians 13, Romans 8. Even though Paul disdained eloquence as valuable in itself, he wrote his inspired epistles in inspiring language. While a painting such as Rembrandt's "Christ at Emmaeus" can leave us speechless, anyone who generalizes that "a picture is worth a thousand words" has never tried to capture John 3:16 (a twenty-five–word sentence) in a picture.[1]

There are bright words as brilliant as a tropic sunrise,

1. Kyle Haselden, *The Urgency of Preaching*, p. 26.

and there are drab words as unattractive as an anemic woman. There are hard words that punch like a prize fighter and weak words as insipid as tea made with one dunk of a tea bag. There are pillow words that comfort people and steel-cold words that threaten them. Some words transplant a listener, at least for an instant, close to the courts of God, and other words send him to the gutter. We live by words, love by words, pray with words, and die for words. Joseph Conrad exaggerated only slightly when he declared, "Give me the right word and the right accent, and I will move the world!"

"But language is not my gift," protests a one-talent servant in the process of burying his ministry. Gift or not, we must use words, and the only question is whether we will use them poorly or well. If a minister will do the sweaty labor, he can become more skillful with them than he is. If he compares himself with C. S. Lewis, Malcolm Muggeridge, or James S. Stewart, he may feel like declaring bankruptcy. Let artisans like these provide ideals toward which he can reach, but in every sermon any minister can be clear and exact in what he says.

Our choice of words is called *style*. Everyone possesses style—be it bland, dull, invigorating, precise—but however we handle or manhandle words becomes our style. Style reflects how we think and how we look at life. Style varies with different speakers, and a speaker will alter his style for different audiences and occasions. Speaking to a high-school class, for instance, permits a style different from that used in addressing a Sunday-morning congregation. The polished wording used in a baccalaureate sermon would sound completely out of place in a small-group Bible study.

While rules governing lucid writing also apply to the sermon, a sermon is not an essay on its hind legs. Since what he writes serves only as a broad preparation for what he will actually say, the manuscript is not a preacher's final product. A sermon should not be read to a congregation. Reading kills the lively sense of communication. Neither should it be memorized. Not only does memorization place a hefty burden on the preacher who speaks several times a week, but an audience senses when a speaker reads words from the wall of his mind. Let a preacher agonize with thought and words at his desk, and what he writes will be internalized. Then let him rehearse several times aloud from the outline, or his memory of the outline, making no conscious effort to recall his exact manuscript at all. When he steps into the pulpit, the written text will have done its work on the preacher's sense of language. Much of the wording will come back to him as he preaches, but not all. In the heat of delivery, sentence structure will change, new phrases will occur to him, and his speech will sparkle like spontaneous conversation. A manuscript, therefore, contributes to the thought and style of the sermon, but it does not dictate it.

Writing a sermon differs from writing a book. A preacher must write as though he were talking with someone, and as in conversation he must strive for immediate understanding. An author knows the reader need not grasp an idea instantly. She can examine a page at leisure, reflect on what she has read, argue with the ideas, and move along at any rate she finds comfortable. Should she stumble across an unfamiliar word, she can pick herself up and consult a dictionary. If she loses an author's path of thought, she can retrace it. In short the reader controls the experience. A listener cannot afford the luxury of leisurely reflection; he cannot go back to listen a second time. If he does not take in what is said as it is said, he will miss it completely. Should he take time out to review the speaker's argument, he will miss what the preacher is saying now. A listener sits at the mercy of the speaker, and the speaker, unlike the writer, must make himself understood instantly.

Several techniques help the preacher think with fierceness and speak with clarity. Some ministers indent and label their manuscripts according to their outlines. By doing this they imprint on their minds the coordination and subordination of their thought. In addition because transitions carry a heavy burden in spoken communication, they take up more space in a sermon manuscript. The listener hears the sermon not as an outline but only as a series of sentences. Transitions stand as road signs to point out where the sermon has been and where it is going and therefore are longer and more detailed than in writing. Major transitions remind the listener of the subject or the central idea of the sermon; they will review the major points already covered and show how the points relate to the major idea and to each other; and they introduce the next point. As a result of the work they do, major transitions can take up a paragraph or more. Minor transitions linking subpoints may be shorter: sometimes a single word *(therefore, besides, yet, consequently)*, at other places a phrase *(in addition, what is more, as a result of this)*, not unusually a sentence or two. While an author may imply transitions, a speaker develops them. Clear, full, definite transitions look clumsy on paper, but run easily in a sermon and enable a congregation to think the preacher's thoughts with him.

A Clear Style

179

What characteristics of style should a preacher cultivate? First of all he must be clear. Talleyrand once remarked that language was invented to conceal, not reveal, the thoughts of men. Educated people sometimes speak as though Talleyrand had been their speech instructor. They attempt to impress their audience with the profundity of their thought through the obscurity of their language. A sermon is not deep because it is muddy. Whatever has been thought through can be stated simply and clearly. Poincaré, the brilliant French mathematician, insisted, "No man knows anything about higher mathematics until he can explain it clearly to the man on the street!" Similarly no preacher understands a passage in the Bible or a point of theology unless he can express it clearly to the congregation sitting before him.

For the preacher clarity is a moral matter. If what we

preach either draws people to God or keeps them away from Him, then for God's sake and the people's sake we must be clear. Helmut Theilicke reminds us that offense comes not because people do not understand but because they understand all too well, or at least are afraid they will have to understand.[2] Imagine a mass meeting in Russia with a Communist launching a tirade against Christianity. Someone jumps to his feet and shouts, "Jesus is the Messiah!" The audience is startled, and he is ejected for disturbing the meeting. But what if he had cried out: "Jesus Christ is God! He is the only Lord, and all who make the system into a god will go to hell along with their Communist leaders!" He would risk being torn to pieces by the crowd. Clarity reveals the offense of the gospel. It also provides life and hope.

Clear Outline

How then do we bring clarity to our sermons? Clear manuscripts grow out of clear outlines. Communication originates in the mind; not in the fingers, not in the mouth, but in the head. Some preachers have jerky minds. Although they have stimulating insights, their thought follows no natural sequence, and their zigzag thinking runs listeners to death. After a bewildering half-hour trying to keep up with a jerky speaker, listening to a dull friend comes as a soothing relief, like taking a cat in your lap after holding a squirrel. Zigzag thinking can be straightened out only by outlining the overall thought before working on details. Laboring over a paragraph or sentence is pointless unless the preacher knows what he wants it to say. Clear manuscripts develop from clear outlines.

Short Sentences

Furthermore, to be clear one must keep sentences short. Rudolf Flesch in *The Art of Plain Talk* insists that clarity

---

2. *Encounter with Spurgeon*, p. 34.

increases as sentence length decreases. According to his formula a clear writer will average about seventeen or eighteen words to a sentence and will not allow any sentence to wander over thirty words.[3] In the sermon manuscript short sentences keep the thought from tangling and therefore are easier for the preacher to remember. When he delivers his sermon, the minister will not concern himself at all with sentence length, just as he does not think about commas, periods, or exclamation points. In making himself understood, his words tumble out in long, short, even broken sentences, punctuated by pauses, vocal slides, and variations in pitch, rate, and force. While the short sentences in the manuscript serve his mind, they have little to do with his delivery.

Simple Sentence Structure

Keep sentence structure simple. A clearer, more energetic style emerges when we follow the thinking sequence: main subject, main verb, and (where needed) main object. In the jargon of grammarians, concentrate on the independent clause before adding dependent clauses. (An independent clause can stand alone as a complete sentence; a dependent clause cannot.) If we start into a sentence without pinning down what we want to emphasize, we usually end up stressing insignificant details. If we add too many dependent clauses, we complicate our sentences, making them harder to understand and remember. Style will be clearer if we package one thought in one sentence. For two thoughts use two sentences. Arthur Schopenhauer scolded the Germans: "If it is an impertinent thing to interrupt another person when he is speaking, it is no less impertinent to interrupt yourself." Complicated sentences have an additional disadvantage. They slow the pace of a sermon. As Henry Ward Beecher put it, "A switch with leaves on it doesn't tingle."

---

3. Pp. 38–39.

Simple Words

Simple words also contribute to a clear style. Ernest T. Campbell tells of the wag who in a moment of frustration declared, "Every profession is a conspiracy against the layman."[4] Any citizen who has battled with an income-tax return wonders why the Internal Revenue Service cannot say what it means. Lawyers assure themselves of a place by embalming the law in "legalese." Scientists keep the little man at bay by resorting to symbols and language only the initiates understand. Theologians and ministers too seem to keep themselves in jobs by resorting to language that bewilders ordinary mortals. Beware of jargon. Specialized vocabulary helps professionals within a discipline to communicate, but it becomes jargon when used unnecessarily. While it takes three years to get through seminary, it can take ten years to get over it. If a preacher peppers his sermons with words like *eschatology, angst, pneumatology, exegesis, existential, Johannine*, he throws up barriers to communication. Jargon combines the pretentiousness of "big" words with the deadness of a cliché, and it is often used to impress rather than inform an audience.

182

Use a short word unless a longer word is absolutely necessary. Josh Billings strikes a blow for simplicity and clarity when he says, "Young man, when you search Webster's dictionary to find words big enough to convey your meaning, you can make up your mind you don't mean much." Long words have paralysis in their tails. Legend has it that a few years ago a young copywriter came up with an ad for a new kind of soap: "The alkaline element and fats in this product are blended in such a way as to secure the highest quality of saponification, along with a specific gravity that keeps it on top of the water, relieving the bather of the trouble and annoyance of fishing around for it at the bottom of the tub during his ablution." A more experienced ad man captured the

---

4. *Locked in a Room with Open Doors* (Waco, Tex.: Word, 1974), p. 46.

same idea in two simple words: "It floats." George G. Williams maintains that from 70 to 78 percent of the words used by W. Somerset Maugham, Sinclair Lewis, Robert Louis Stevenson, and Charles Dickens have only one syllable.[5] Seventy-three percent of the words in Psalm 23, 76 percent of the words in the Lord's Prayer, and 80 percent of the words in I Corinthians 13 are one-syllable words.

No matter how accurately a phrase or word expresses a speaker's meaning, it is worthless if the listeners do not know what it means. "Speak," said Abraham Lincoln, "so that the most lowly can understand you, and the rest will have no difficulty." Billy Sunday, the noted evangelist, understood the value of simplicity when he said:

> If a man were to take a piece of meat and smell it and look disgusted, and his little boy were to say, "What's the matter with it, Pop?" and he were to say, "It is undergoing a process of decomposition in the formation of new chemical compounds," the boy would be all in. But if the father were to say, "It's rotten," then the boy would understand and hold his nose. *Rotten* is a good Anglo-Saxon word, and you do not have to go to a dictionary to find out what it means.[6]

This does not mean that a minister should talk down to his congregation. Instead his rule of thumb should be: Don't overestimate the people's vocabulary or underestimate their intelligence.

A Direct and Personal Style

In addition to being clear, a second major characteristic of style is that it must be direct and personal. While writing is addressed "to whom it may concern," a sermon is delivered to the men and women of the First Baptist Church meeting on July 15 near Ninth and Elm Streets at eleven o'clock in

---

5. *Creative Writing for Advanced College Classes*, p. 106.
6. In John R. Pelsma, *Essentials of Speech*, p. 193.

the morning. The writer and reader sit alone, distant from each other and unknown. The preacher speaks to his hearers face to face and calls them by name. Written language communicates the results of thinking, while spoken language represents a spontaneity of thought that Donald C. Bryant and Karl R. Wallace describe as "vivid-realization-of-idea-at-the-moment-of-utterance."[7] Therefore a sermon must not sound like a thesis read to a congregation. It sounds like conversation where thinking is going on and where the preacher talks to and with his hearers. Speaker and listener sense they are in touch with each other.

The sermon uses the style of direct address. While a writer might say, "In his conversation the Christian must be careful of how he speaks about others," a preacher will more likely say, "You must be careful of how you talk about others." The personal pronoun *you* gives both minister and audience a sense of oneness. While *you* can be effective, at other times the preacher will say *we* because he means "you and I." The *we* of direct address stands in contrast to the editorial *we* that substitutes for the pronoun *I*. An editorial *we* sounds as if the preacher speaks for a committee. The *we* of oral style, like the *we* of good conversation, means "you and I together."

A speaker will use questions where a writer may not. The question invites a listener to think about what the preacher will say next and often introduces a major point or new idea. It may invite the congregation to respond to what the preacher has said and is often employed to conclude a sermon. Questions show clearly that the audience and speaker are face to face.

Personal style pays little attention to the conventions of formal writing. Contractions present no problem *(can't, we'll, wouldn't),* and neither do split infinitives. What is appropriate in good conversation fits preaching. This does not mean, of course, that anything goes. Poor grammar or faulty pronun-

---

7. *Fundamentals of Public Speaking,* 3d ed., p. 129.

ciation unnerve a listener, like a giggle in a prayer meeting, and raise doubts about a preacher's competence.

Slang gets mixed reviews. When used deliberately, slang can capture attention and inject a feeling of casualness and informality into the sermon. When used thoughtlessly, slang sounds trite and even cheap and betrays a lazy mind. Personal, direct speech does not call for careless speech or undignified English. The language of effective preaching should be the language of a gentleman in conversation.

A Vivid Style

A third characteristic of effective style is vividness. Wayne C. Minnick argues that communication which taps a listener's experience appeals to both mind and feelings. We learn about the world around us through hearing, sight, smell, taste, and touch. To get an audience to experience the message, therefore, a minister must appeal to the senses.[8] A preacher does this directly through sight and sound. The congregation sees his gestures and facial expressions and hears what he says. He also stimulates the senses indirectly through his use of words. Language makes listeners recall impressions of past experiences and respond to the words as they did to the event. For example, gastric juices flow when we hear the words *hot, buttered bread* and stop in a shudder when we think of roaches crawling on it. In doing this, the speaker enables people to connect an experience they have not had with feelings they have had.

Vividness increases when you use specific, concrete details and plenty of them. We label a phrase "specific" if it is explicit and exact, and "concrete" if it paints pictures on the mind. The figure $1,923,212.92 is specific down to the penny but not concrete. The figure $275 on your monthly electric bill is concrete. You can't visualize the first figure, but you

185

---

8. *The Art of Persuasion*, chap. 7.

can the second. Specific details add interest if they are concrete. They communicate because they relate to the experiences of the audience. Therefore instead of "produce" say
"cabbages, cucumbers, and oranges." Rather than "weapon"
say "heavy lead pipe." In place of "major cities" be specific:
"New York, Chicago, Dallas, or San Francisco." The following statement is abstract: "In the course of human experience, we observe that the events of our existence have definite
cyclical characteristics. Awareness of these will direct the
observer to a high degree of appropriateness in his actions."
The preacher in Ecclesiastes expressed that same thought
this way: "For everything there is a season, and a time for
every purpose under heaven: a time to be born, and a time
to die; . . . a time to weep, and a time to laugh; a time to
mourn, and a time to dance; . . . a time to keep silence, and
a time to speak" (3:1–7 ASV).

Like an artist or novelist a minister must learn to think
in pictures. That means he must visualize details. Gustave
Flaubert gave his writing disciple Guy de Maupassant an assignment: "You go down to the [railroad] station and you will
find there about fifty cabs. They all look pretty much alike,
but they are not alike. You pick out one and describe it so
accurately that when it goes past I cannot possibly mistake
it."[9] Concrete language develops first as a way of seeing and
then as a way of writing and speaking. Unless we observe
life, we cannot represent it clearly.

Vividness develops when we let nouns and verbs carry
our meaning. Adjectives and adverbs clutter speech and keep
company with weak words. According to E. B. White, "The
adjective hasn't been built that can pull a weak or inaccurate
noun out of a tight place." Strong nouns and verbs stand
alone. A "tall man" should become a "giant"; a "large bird"
a "pelican." Say "he bellowed," not "he talked loudly"; or "he
trotted" rather than "he went quickly." Be especially careful

---

9. In Christian Gauss, *The Papers of Christian Gauss*, ed. Katherine Gauss
Jackson and Hiram Haydn (New York: Random, 1957), p. 145.

of qualifiers like *very, so, quite, rather, too.* They betray a failure to choose words of substance. "Scalding" has strength, "very hot" does not; "excruciating" hurts more than "too painful"; and "scintillating" paints a better picture than "so interesting." When choosing verbs use live ones. Finite active verbs make sentences go. The principle to follow is "Somebody does something." Passive verbs suck the life out of speech. "Opinions and judgments are formed by us on the basis of what we have known" sounds dead. "We think as we have known" possesses vitality. "A good time was had by all" lies there while "Everyone enjoyed himself" moves.

Verbs, like nouns, wake up the imagination when they are precise. He "went" gets him there but not as clearly as "crawled," "stumbled," "shuffled," "lurched." She "shouts," "shrieks," "rants," "whispers" tells us what "says" does not.

Vividness also increases when you employ fresh figures of speech. Metaphors and similes produce sensations in the listener or cause him to recall images of previous experiences. Alexander Maclaren stimulates the sense of touch when he says, "All sin is linked together in a slimy tangle like a field of seaweed so that a man once caught in its oozy fingers is almost sure to drown." George Byron appeals to sight when he tells us:

187

> *The Assyrian came down like the wolf on the fold,*
> *and his cohorts all gleaming in silver and gold.*

Charles H. Spurgeon captured the senses in a simile that refers to a past era "when the great universe lay in the mind of God like unborn forests in the acorn's cup." Alfred North Whitehead called up an image when he reflected, "Knowledge doesn't keep any better than fish." Figures of speech conserve time by packing more into a phrase than a word-wasting speaker expresses in a paragraph. Consider a few:

fig-leaf phrases that cover naked ignorance
words that have been hollowed out on the inside and
    filled with whipped cream
clichés that fall like tombstones over dead ideas

If Protestantism is found dead, the sermon will be the
dagger in her heart.

He avoided the sticky issues as though he were stepping
around puddles of hot tar.

Metaphors and similes, like lobsters, must be served fresh.
Both the literal and figurative meanings should strike the
mind at the same instant. When the literal image fades because the comparison has been overworked, the figure loses
its force. The listener becomes tone deaf to them. The following once hit like a one-two punch but now hardly touch us
at all:

outreach of the church
tried and true
lost and dying world
born-again Christian
saving souls
souls for your hire
listeners in radio land
prayer-hearing and prayer-answering God
straddle the fence

When a comparison has turned stale, throw it out and come
up with a fresh one that clarifies the point and keeps the
audience alert. Relevance shows up in style as well as content. We must speak the eternal message in today's words. A
minister should study magazine ads and radio and television
commercials for easily understood language that speaks to
captives of our culture. Common observation tells us what
linguistic tests have proved—much of the language used in
our pulpits is "imprecise, irrelevant, and insignificant."[10]

Effective style cannot be taught like a mathematical formula. Mastery of "the well-dressed word" requires an eye for
particulars and a search for significant resemblances between things not ordinarily associated with one another. In
short, doing away with hackneyed and tired speech demands
imagination. In expository preaching nothing has been more

10. Donald O. Soper, *The Advocacy of the Gospel*, p. 36.

needed—and more lacking. Expositors who represent the creative God dare not become, in Robert Browning's description, "clods untouched by a spark."

How can you shun the sin of sounding uninteresting?

1. *Pay attention to your own use of language.* In private conversation don't shift your mind into neutral and use phrases that idle rather than jump. Cultivate the choice of fresh comparisons, and you will find them easier to use when you preach. Beecher gives this testimony about illustrations that also applies to style: ". . . while illustrations are as natural to me as breathing, I use fifty now to one in the early years of my ministry. . . . I developed a tendency that was latent in me, and educated myself in that respect; and that, too, by study and practice, by hard thought, and by a great many trials, both with the pen, and extemporaneously by myself, when I was walking here and there."[11]

2. *Study how others use language.* When a writer or speaker shakes you awake, examine how he did it. Since poetry bursts with similes and metaphors, studying verse develops a feel for figurative language.

3. *Read aloud.* Reading aloud does two things for you. First, your vocabulary will increase. As children we learned to speak by listening and imitating long before we could read or write. Reading aloud re-creates that experience. Second, as you read style better than your own, new patterns of speech and creative wording will be etched on your nervous system. You will develop a feel for picture-making language. Read to your wife and children so that you will be forced to interpret what you read. Read novels, plays, sermons, and especially the Bible. The King James Version presents God's truth in Shakespearean grandeur, and the New International Version puts it in more up-to-date dress. Both have impressive style.

---

11. *Yale Lectures on Preaching*, p. 175.

New Concepts

Style
Characteristics of effective sermon style
    clear
    direct and personal
    vivid

Definitions

Style — the choice of words.

Chapter 10

How to Preach So People Will Listen

Most books on homiletics say a great deal about the development of sermons but little about their delivery. Pastors appear to take a lead from these preaching texts. While a minister spends hours every week on sermon construction, he seldom gives even a few hours a year to thinking about delivery. Yet sermons do not come into the world as outlines or manuscripts. They live only when preached. A sermon ineptly delivered arrives stillborn.

The effectiveness of our sermons depends on two factors: what we say and how we say it. Both are important. Apart from life-related, biblical content we have nothing worth communicating; but without skillful delivery, we will not get our content across to the congregation. In order of significance the ingredients making up a sermon are thought, arrangement, language, voice, and gesture. In priority of impressions, however, the order reverses. Gesture and voice emerge as the most obvious and determinative. Every empirical study of delivery and its effect on the outcome of a speech or sermon arrives at an identical conclusion: delivery matters a great deal.[1]

Not only do the speaker's voice and gestures first strike the audience's senses, but his inflections and actions transmit his feelings and attitudes more accurately than his words. During the 1970s scholars in several disciplines—psychology, anthropology, sociology, and speech communication, to name a few—investigated the effects of nonverbal communication. These researchers observed how we broadcast messages by the way we sit or stand, by facial expressions, by gestures, and even by how much space we allow between ourselves and those we meet.[2] As a by-product of these studies, several paperbacks promised to interpret this silent language so that readers could use it for personal advantage. The "overclaim" of these books probably produced as many skeptics as believers. Individual and cultural differences in nonverbal communication make dogmatic definitions of the meaning of body language simplistic and possibly dangerous. For example, to assert that arms folded across the chest reveals that an individual wants to shut out those around her is like saying that the word *model* always refers to a small-scale replica of a larger object.

Yet no observant person would seriously deny that we communicate messages even when we do not speak. Friends believe that one measure of the depth of their relationship lies in their ability to understand each other even when they sit together silently. We determine that casual acquaintances,

---

1. Wayne N. Thompson, *Quantitative Research in Public Address and Communication*, p. 83.

2. See, for example, *Journal of Communication* 22 (1972): 335–476. This entire issue (no. 4) deals with nonverbal communication; individual articles on the subject appear in this journal regularly. See too Robert Rosenthal et al., "Body Talk and Tone of Voice: The Language Without Words," *Psychology Today* 8 (September 1974): 64–68; or Ernst G. Beier, "Nonverbal Communication: How We Send Emotional Messages," *Psychology Today* 8 (October 1974): 53–56.

or even strangers, are friendly, angry, or worried by their posture, facial expressions, or tone of voice. Smiles, frowns, stares, winks, or glances affect whether we like or dislike, trust or distrust those we meet. The writer of Proverbs understood the power of nonverbal communication when he declared: "A worthless person, a wicked man, is one who walks with a false mouth, who winks with his eyes, who signals with his feet, who points with his fingers; who with perversity in his heart devises evil continually, who spreads strife" (Prov. 6:12–14 NASB). The eyes, hands, face, and feet say as much to a congregation as the words we utter—in fact more. Psychologist Albert Mehrabian breaks it down to a formula. Only 7 percent of the impact of a speaker's message comes through his words; 38 percent springs from his voice, 55 percent from facial expressions.[3]

Several observations can be drawn from this research that relate to preachers and preaching. First, nonverbal language possesses strategic importance in public speaking. When we address a congregation, three different communication networks operate at the same time: our words, our intonation, and our gestures. All three communicate ideas. When actor George Arliss first read the play *Disraeli,* he advised the author to take out two pages. "I can say that with a look," he said. "What look?" asked the author. Arliss demonstrated, and the pages came out.[4] In fact actions may often be more expressive than words. To place the finger on the lips says more than "Be quiet." Opening the eyes and raising the eyebrows expresses surprise that words cannot, and a shrug of the shoulders communicates an idea that is beyond words. In general, though, nonverbal elements more frequently communicate emotions and attitudes. Edward T. Hall sums up the findings of social scientists when he observes, "In addition to what we say with our verbal language, we are

---

3. In Flora Davis, "How to Read Body Language."

4. In Loren D. Reid, *Speaking Well,* p. 141.

constantly communicating our real feelings in our silent language—the language of behavior."[5]

Second, research and experience agree that if nonverbal messages contradict the verbal, listeners will more likely believe the silent language. It seems more difficult to lie with the whole body than with the lips alone. This is the thrust of Sigmund Freud's observation: "No mortal can keep a secret. If his lips are silent, he chatters with his fingertips; betrayal oozes out of him at every pore." A pastor's words may insist, "This is important," but if his voice sounds flat and expressionless and his body stands limp, the congregation will not believe him. If a preacher shakes his fist at his hearers while he says in scolding tones, "What this church needs is more love and deep concern for each other!" the people in the pew will wonder whether he knows what he is talking about. Since a vast amount of preaching involves attitudes that either reinforce or contradict what our words proclaim, a preacher dare not ignore delivery.

Third, effective delivery begins with desires. The philosopher-humorist Abe Martin suggested, "There is more difference between a professional and an amateur than anything else on earth!" In public speaking the amateur says words. The professional, on the other hand, possesses a deep desire to communicate. The amateur settles for getting his ideas out of his head, while the professional strives to get them into ours. In the preacher technical knowledge and training in the art of public address cannot take the place of conviction and responsibility. Having something to say to a congregation that you want them to understand and live by provides the essential stimulus for good delivery. It produces the emotional "set" for speaking. Therefore good delivery from the pulpit resembles lively conversation. When we concentrate on ideas to make others understand and accept them, delivery comes naturally. It does not emerge from slavishly following a set of rules. Charles R. Brown in his Yale lectures

5. *The Silent Language*, p. 10.

on preaching described the pulpit work of George Macdonald in London:

> He read for the Scripture lesson that morning the eleventh chapter of Hebrews. When the time came for the sermon, [he] said: "You have all heard about these men of faith. I shall not try to tell you what faith is—there are theological professors who can do that much better than I could do it. I am here to help you to believe." Then followed such a simple, heartfelt, and majestic manifestation of the man's own faith in those unseen realities which are eternal, as to beget faith in the minds and hearts of all his hearers. His heart was in his work, and his delivery was effective because it rested back upon the genuine beauty of his own inner life.[6]

"His heart was in his work." No rules can take the place of that. Sincerity, enthusiasm, and deep earnestness tear down barriers that allow the real self to break free. In that sense effective delivery approximates the everyday give-and-take of conversation.

Saying that pulpit delivery resembles conversation, however, does not mean that our ordinary ways of speaking are necessarily our best ways. How we talk in private develops from an accumulation of lifelong habits. We can acquire poor habits of communication just as we develop bad habits of posture or eating. What is more, some behavior inconspicuous in private situations becomes distressingly obvious in public speaking. When we address an audience, our position becomes unique and emphatic. Stuffing hands in the pockets, stroking the hair or face, playing with a ring, fussing with a necktie, shuffling the feet are the bad grammar of delivery. Mannerisms and repetitious behavior peculiar to you may go unnoticed by friends and be tolerated by associates, but in the pulpit they scream for attention and divert people from what you are saying. In the pulpit, therefore, movement of the body must be disciplined to be effective.

---

6. *The Art of Preaching*, p. 170.

At first, attempts to improve delivery often feel unnatural. The novice may insist that he should abandon the effort since a minister is not an actor and working on delivery violates his personality. But acquiring any habit usually involves initial self-consciousness. When we first drive an automobile or take up tennis, for example, we feel awkward as we try to control our behavior. After practice and experience, however, the self-consciousness disappears and the new-learned behavior comes easily. It takes effort and discipline to seem natural before an audience.

What are some nonverbal factors in delivery to which we should give our attention?

Grooming and Dress

When the apostle Paul declared that he would "become all things to all men, that I might by all means save some" (I Cor. 9:22 NKJB), he established a basic tenet of Christian communication. In matters of moral indifference, what matters most is not my feelings but the feelings and attitudes of others. Since grooming and dress make a difference in how a listener responds to us, they should make a difference to us.

A basic rule of grooming and dress for the preacher is that they should fit the audience, the situation, and the speaker. For instance, changing fashions in hair styles, beards, sideburns, and moustaches make absolute rules impossible. A minister aware of his community and its standards will not want to allow his hair to stand in the way of his ministry. John T. Molloy, wardrobe consultant to many of America's top corporations, has been asked if any traits are common to all successful executives. He singles out two: their hair is combed and their shoes are shined. And they expect the same of other men, particularly subordinates. Molloy's studies indicate that disheveled hair, even if it is short, triggers strong negative reactions in other men. Hair, whatever its length, should be neat.[7]

A program of regular exercise and proper diet can trim off excess pounds that hinder communication. It is hard to believe that a minister thirty pounds overweight takes seriously the biblical injunctions about self-control. Grooming also includes the use of deodorants, toothpaste, and breath fresheners. While television commercials make bad breath sound worse than cancer, breath odor and body odor nonetheless can be offenses that build walls where we want bridges.

Recent research demonstrates that dress and appearance cause us to make judgments about others without really being aware of why we make those judgments. Apparently the old saw "Clothes make the man" should be revised to say "Clothes express the man." While we may dress to be comfortable, clothes should make others comfortable with us as well. *Psychology Today* reported on a three-month study done with seven salesmen to determine the influence of dress on sales: "At a time when jeans and safari jackets are turning up in even the most sedate establishments, does wearing a business suit matter anymore? In some businesses, it evidently does. When salesmen in a Montgomery, Alabama, men's store wore suits,...the average value of their sales was 43 percent higher than when they wore shirtsleeves and a tie, and 60 percent higher than when they wore an open-collar shirt."[8]

Pastors who feel inadequate in selecting the best wardrobe for their budget would be wise to put themselves in the hands of an experienced clothier in their area. His counsel on clothes can save money and turn a liability into an asset. Suits should be kept clean and pressed. Socks should cover the leg; pockets should not bulge with a collection of pens, datebooks, eyeglasses, and a wallet; and a fresh shirt should

---

7. *Dress for Success* (New York: Wyden, 1975).

8. Margot Slade, "Casual Clothes Are the Death of a Salesman," *Psychology Today* 13 (August 1979): 29.

be adorned with a neatly tied tie. Handkerchiefs displayed should not be limp, or if carried in the pocket, they should be clean. A minister does not prove he is an expository preacher by looking as though he dressed staring into a Greek text instead of a mirror.

Movement and Gestures

God designed the human body to move. If a congregation wants to look at a statue, they can go to a museum. Even there, however, the most impressive statues are those that appear alive. In most realms the professional uses his whole body. The conductor of a symphony, the concert pianist, the baseball pitcher, the umpire, the actor, and the golfer all put their bodies into what they do. An accomplished speaker likewise lets his body speak for him.

Content should motivate movement. This principle applies in two ways. Some ministers need to move. They stand almost motionless before their people, little more than talking heads that refuse to let their bodies interact with the message. Such men need to set their bodies free to do what their minds and emotions demand. They should not inhibit the physical expressions that accompany vigorous thought. A preacher needs to carry over into preaching the same freedom he gives to his hands, arms, and head in personal conversation. While some of us gesture more than others, we should not gesture less in the pulpit than we do in private. In fact we need to make our gestures larger, more forceful and deliberate.

The principle that content should motivate movement also means that some speakers should move less. If they pace back and forth, they reveal their uneasiness and their movement disturbs the listener's concentration. Their actions do not spring from content, they merely discharge nervous energy. While their walking benefits them, it does little for the congregation. If your movement comes from habit, stand still.

If it comes from content, drop your inhibitions and express it. For example, when you introduce a new point in your sermon, you may take a step or two from where you are standing to show visually the transition in thought. When that idea has been developed and you proceed to another, then you can move back to your original position again. If you want the listeners to relax after a major point, you may step back and pause. Hamlet's instruction to his actors still holds: "Suit the action to the word, the word to the action."

A specific part of total bodily movement is gestures that relate to speaking as diagrams do to a book. Gestures are for expression and not exhibition, and they communicate in several ways. Gestures help us explain and describe. If a preacher wants to depict the walls of Babylon, he can do so more effectively if he gestures as he describes them. Think of the following description without gestures, and then with gestures: "Babylon stood as a monument to pagan power. The city was surrounded by an intricate system of double walls; the outer range covered seventeen miles and was strong and wide enough for chariots to pass on top. These massive walls were buttressed by giant defense towers and pierced by eight large gates."

Gestures emphasize our speech. Contrast saying "This is extremely important" with your hands hanging limply by your side and then with a clenched fist shaken at the word *extremely*. The gesture injects vigor into your voice. In giving emphasis, if you must pound, pound softly; and don't shake your finger at your audience. That action scolds your listeners.

Gestures maintain interest and hold attention. A moving object captures the eye more than one at rest.

Gestures put the speaker at ease. When your body works to reinforce your ideas, you feel more confident and alert.

Gestures help our listeners experience what we feel as they identify with us. At a football game fans cringe when their favorite runner falls victim to a crushing tackle; sometimes they actually kick the seat below them while watching a crucial field goal attempt. This projective behavior is called *empathy.* In essence empathy is sympathetic, muscular response in which your listeners, in a limited way, act with you. Because those subliminal actions tap feelings, listeners feel what you feel and hopefully what you wish them to feel about your ideas. If a speaker fidgets or fails to control his gestures, his actions reflect his discomfort. The audience may squirm or in some other way empathize with those actions, feeling uncomfortable too. On the other hand if through your gestures you can get your congregation to act and feel in a manner appropriate to your thought and purpose—even though this takes place on a subconscious level—you increase the likelihood of winning a positive hearing for your message.[9]

Spontaneous Gestures

What are some characteristics of expressive gestures? First, gestures should be spontaneous. Gesture but don't "make gestures." Gestures should develop from within as the outgrowth of conviction and feeling. While gestures can be practiced, they should not be planned. If in preaching the sermon they do not come naturally, let them go.

Definite Gestures

Gestures should also be definite. When you make a gesture, make it. A half-hearted gesture communicates nothing positive. Put your body behind it. A simple gesture with the index finger involves not only the finger, hand, and wrist, but the upper arm, shoulder, and back as well. Even your weight shifts slightly to give added force. If a gesture appears awkward, it may be that the entire body does not support it.

Varied Gestures

Gestures should be varied. Repetition of a single gesture, even a spontaneous and forceful one, calls attention to itself

---

9. See Jon Eisenson and Paul H. Boase, *Basic Speech*, pp. 334–35.

and irritates an audience. For instance, a pump-handle gesture gains emphasis, but used too often it looks like it needs a well. Stand in front of a mirror and note how many different ways you can use your body. Someone who has bothered to count them insists that we can produce 700,000 distinct elementary signs with our arms, wrists, hands, and fingers.[10] Try using either hand, both hands, an open hand, a closed hand, palm up, palm down. Experiment with the arms, head, eyes, face.

Properly Timed Gestures

Gestures should be properly timed. The gesture either accompanies or precedes the word or phrase that carries most of your meaning. If the stroke of the gesture follows the word or phrase, then it may look ridiculous. Poorly timed gestures usually reflect a lack of spontaneity and proper motivation.

Eye Contact

As important as grooming and movement are to a speaker, eye contact probably ranks as the most effective single means of nonverbal communication at his disposal. Eyes communicate. They supply feedback and at the same time hold an audience's attention. When you look directly at your hearers, you pick up cues that tell you whether they understand what you are saying, whether they are interested, and whether they enjoy the sermon enough to continue listening. An alert speaker will adjust what he says—for example, adding explanation or illustrations—as he interprets these responses. Moreover listeners feel that ministers who "look them in the eye" want to talk with them personally. Therefore pastors who gaze over the audience's heads, stare down at notes, look

---

10. Richard Paget, *Human Speech: Some Observations, Experiments, and Conclusions as to the Nature, Origin, Purpose, and Possible Improvement of Human Speech.*

out of windows, or, worse, shut their eyes while they speak, place themselves at a crippling disadvantage. Almost without exception a congregation will not listen attentively to a speaker who does not look at them while he talks. Just as significant, people mistrust someone who avoids eye contact, and as a result they undervalue what he says.

Even though you address a congregation as a group, you talk with them as individuals. As you stand to speak, pause to establish personal contact with your hearers. Move your eyes over the congregation and let them rest for an instant on several different people. Throughout the sermon continue your eye contact. Plan to talk with one listener at a time for a second or two, looking that person in the eye, then turn to someone else. Choose listeners in every section of the audi-torium, and keep the eye contact long enough so that they know that you have singled them out and are speaking to them. If the congregation is very large, you can select a small group in one area and look at them for a moment or two, then shift to another group, and continue to do that throughout the sermon. Be sure not only to look at your listeners but to talk with them. Concentrate on communicating to each one the message you eagerly want him to understand.

Your people need to see your face. Therefore illumine the pulpit with a strong light, placed at an angle that keeps your eyes from being thrown into shadow. Take a light meter and test the focus of light in the front of the church. Sunday after Sunday preachers stand in dimly lit pulpits, and the congre-gation has only a shadowy view of his countenance. The pul-pit should be located as close to the listeners as possible, at an angle that makes it easy for them to see the minister's eyes and the full range of emotions playing across his face.

Vocal Delivery

Speech consists of more than words and sentences. The voice conveys ideas and feelings apart from words. We make judgments about a speaker's physical and emotional state— whether he is frightened, angry, fatigued, sick, happy, confident—based on the tremor of his voice, its loudness, rate, and pitch. Since the minister's voice is a major tool in his profession, he should understand how his vocal mechanism works and how to use it skillfully.

The human voice is produced in much the same manner as sound is produced by a wind instrument. Just as the reed in the instrument must vibrate, so must the vocal folds in the larynx when air is expelled from the lungs. Voice begins therefore when a column of air is pumped from the lungs through the bronchial tubes, which connect the lungs to the windpipe. As the exhaled breath moves across the vocal folds in the larynx, located in the upper end of the windpipe, it sets up the vibrations that become sound waves. This sound is then amplified as it vibrates in the larynx, throat, sinuses and mouth. These cavities, called resonators, act somewhat like the hollow section or soundboard of a stringed musical instrument, which increases the volume of sound made by the strings. As the resonating cavities change shape through the movement of the palate, jaws, teeth, lips, tongue, and the back wall of the pharynx, they produce the ultimate quality of the voice. Consonants such as l, p, t, d, s, r are also formed as these movements take place.[11]

203

Even a casual understanding of the vocal mechanism reveals that since tone is produced on the exhaled stream of breath, a good supply of breath, steadily controlled, is essential. Because tone begins by the vibration of the vocal cords, a vocal-cord impulse free from undue strain or tension is also necessary. Since the final sound results from modification in the resonating cavities, attention should be given to the throat, mouth, and nasal resonators.

Most speakers can improve the quality of voice, even without extended drill, if they understand how vocal sounds

---

11. For an extended discussion of the physiological basis of speech, see Giles W. Gray and Claude M. Wise, *The Bases of Speech*, pp. 135– 99.

are made. For example, if you breathe efficiently, you should expand the beltline instead of the chest. A speaker should be able to recite the entire alphabet on a single breath. Some ministers allow the pitch of their voices to rise when they increase their volume. They need to practice going down in pitch when they go up in force. Others muffle their sound by speaking with a tight jaw, lazy tongue, or clenched teeth. Still others allow too much air to escape as they talk, giving the voice a breathy quality. Some ministers speak too rapidly and slur their words, while many speak in a monotone. Most basic texts on speech supply exercises that can correct these common faults.[12] Major universities and many smaller colleges maintain speech clinics, staffed by competent instructors who provide help for speakers with more complex problems. With such assistance available a minister has little excuse for not developing the capability of his voice to the optimum.

A speaker emphasizes what he says in only four ways—by variety in pitch, punch, progress, and pause. The use of these or a combination of them becomes the punctuation of speech.

Pitch

Pitch involves the movement of the voice up and down the scale, in different registers, with various inflections. Sometimes changes in pitch are called melody. If someone asks, with an inflection rising rapidly from low to high pitch, "Do you believe in hell?" he is asking a question. Precisely that same sentence, with a different change in pitch, can imply: "You don't say that you—you of all people—would be so out of touch with modern theology as to believe a medieval superstition like that!" If the individual responds with abrupt downward steps, "I do not," that melody communicates: "No,

12. See, for example, Alan H. Monroe and Douglas Ehninger, *Principles and Types of Speech Communication*, pp. 203–23; or John A. Grasham and Glenn G. Gooder, *Improving Your Speech*.

I don't hold that position. Certainly not. Don't accuse me of such idiocy." While the words don't express disgust, the pitch does.

Monopitch drones us to sleep or wears upon us like a child pounding the same note on the piano. Failure to control pitch effectively is sometimes the reason a preacher's humor falls flat. His listeners cannot tell from his pitch that he is joking.

Punch

Variations in loudness achieve both interest and emphasis. A change in force communicates the relative importance of ideas. In the declaration "The Lord is my shepherd," there are only five words; yet if the sentence is repeated five times and each time a different word is punched, the meaning changes. Entire sections of a sermon can be stressed if a preacher utters them with greater volume.

Unfortunately some preachers know no other way to underline their points, and their sermons sound like shouting sessions. They confuse volume with spiritual power, thinking God speaks only in the whirlwind. Like monopitch, the monotony of unvarying volume wears on a listener. Emphasis comes through variety. Dropping the voice to a near whisper can put an idea into italics as effectively as a loud shout. Intensity can be as effective as volume. Most ministers use only one degree of force when employing a wide range of volume could enhance their delivery.

Progress

Emphasis can also be obtained through changing the rate of delivery. For example, speak David's words of grief over his rebellious son Absalom at the same rate: "Absalom, my son, my son Absalom! Would I had died for thee, O Absalom, my son, my son!" (II Sam. 18:33 ASV). Then speak the sentences very, very slowly. Then speak the first six words rapidly with feeling and the rest slowly. The variety in rate communicates different meanings and emotions.

In the use of rate, as in other means of showing emphasis, the secret lies in contrast. As you recite a story, give out facts, or summarize a passage, you usually do so at a lively pace. Then when you come to a key statement or a major point, you can slow down so that the congregation will appreciate its importance. The sentences spoken more slowly stand out because they are in strong contrast to the content surrounding them. While words may also be emphasized by speeding up their delivery, emphasis is more often accomplished by slowing the rate.

Some ministers have gained a reputation for speaking too rapidly when their problem may be that they fail to speak distinctly or to vary their rate.

Pause

"By your silence," said Rudyard Kipling, "you shall speak." The skilled speaker recognizes that pauses serve as commas, semicolons, periods, and exclamation points. Pauses are the punctuation marks of speech. Pauses are "thoughtful silences." They go beyond a stoppage in speech and give the audience a brief opportunity to think, feel, and respond. The first word or phrase uttered after a pause will stand out from what has preceded it. For even stronger emphasis on a word or phrase, one can pause *after* it as well as before it. A pause before the climax of a story increases suspense, and a dramatic pause introduced when a speaker feels deep emotion can communicate feelings more effectively than words. Pauses not motivated by thought or feeling, however, confuse a listener, just as random punctuation bewilders a reader.

Many speakers are afraid of silence. They do not have enough self-control to pause for long. They feel they must keep talking so that the audience will not think they have forgotten what they want to say. Rather than pause, therefore, they hurry on with an unremitting stream of words — or

worse, fill their sermons with word whiskers such as *er —
and —uh —so —uh.* In some religious circles "Amen" and
"Praise God" are thrown in aimlessly and serve as nothing
more than vocalized pauses. These meaningless sounds and
words communicate nothing; instead they draw attention
away from the idea and irritate the congregation.

A pause seldom seems as long to the listener as it does
to the speaker. If you concentrate fiercely on your thought
and feel the emotion of what you are saying, a pause will
underline important points. While you pause, continue to look
at your listeners intently. Audiences sense when a speaker is
thinking hard, and they will wait with him. A few speakers
may misuse the technique and, by pausing too long, sound
melodramatic. The pause should be long enough to call attention to the thought but not so long that the silence calls
attention to the pause.

The minister should rehearse his sermon before he delivers it. Rehearsal tests the structure of the message. The progress of thought that seemed clear on paper may feel awkward
when the material is spoken. As he says his sermon aloud, a
preacher may change the progression of ideas into a pattern
that flows more easily.

Rehearsal also enhances style. As he practices, the
preacher may find a phrase that illuminates an idea in a particularly effective way. He should not rehearse in order to
memorize the sermon (he should not hesitate to alter some
words or phrases once in the pulpit). Rather he should work
to have a clear progression of thought and to express it in
language that communicates what he wants to say.

Rehearsal also improves delivery. A professional actor
would not think of going before an audience without first
going over his material orally—usually many times—to be
sure that it comes to him easily. How can it be spoken so that
it will be clear? When should he increase his force, vary his
rate, change his pitch, or pause to let a line sink in? While a
preacher is more than an actor, he should not be less. Effective delivery must be practiced since the minister cannot think

about it much as he speaks. The good habits acquired in the study will come more easily in the pulpit. Beginners will profit from rehearsing with a full voice while standing before a mirror and using a tape recorder. More experienced speakers may settle for sotto voce or no voice as they go over their sermons. For a few, sitting and thinking through their sermons, animated in their imaginations by a picture of themselves before the congregation, will be enough. For all of us, having traveled a path before makes it simpler to follow that path again.

New Concepts

Nonverbal language

Definitions

Nonverbal language—gestures, facial expression, and tone
of voice that transmit messages.

Appendix 1

Answers to Exercises

Exercises in Chapter 2

1. **Subject:** The test of a good sermon
   Complement: It reveals what you are.
2. **Subject:** Why the modern pulpit is weak
   Complement: It has ignored the Bible.
3. **Subject:** The consequence of not believing in God
   Complement: We will believe anything.
4. **Subject:** The value of a good reputation
   Complement: It is worth more than material things.
5. **Subject:** Why everyone should praise God
   Complement: We should praise Him for His strong love and eternal faithfulness.
6. **Subject:** Why we need memories (or, the benefit of memories)
   Complement: They keep us from insignificance.
7. **Subject:** How we should deal with others

Complement: We should treat them with the respect one gives to members of one's family.

8. **Subject:** The benefits of walking
Complement: It benefits us physically and psychologically.

9. **Subject:** The current influence of astrology
Complement: It is attracting more adherents and is spreading to places that would ordinarily reject it.

10. **Subject:** The poor reputation of White House food
Complement: The reputation of the White House kitchen is undeserved.

Exercises in Chapter 4

1. **Subject:** Why older people don't learn
Complement: They feel they already know and are too concerned about other matters.
Functional question being addressed: Is it true? (validity)

2. **Subject:** How to listen to the Word of God
Complement: Listen carefully and obey.
Functional question being addressed: So what? What difference does it make? (application)

3. **Subject:** How to help your golf game in the winter
Complement: Practice before a full-length mirror.
Functional question being addressed: Is it true? (validity)

4. **Subject:** The popularity of the CB radio
Complement: It has affected every segment of American life.
Functional question being addressed: Is it true? (validity)

5. **Subject:** How we learn about reality
Complement: We learn by repeated, unconscious experience.
Functional question being addressed: What does it mean? (explanation)

6. **Subject:** The importance of memory in music
Complement: Without it we would have no melody.

Functional question being addressed: What does it mean? (explanation)

7. **Subject:** The positive effect of the Watergate scandal
   Complement: It has delayed the nation's rapid move toward centralized, pervasive government
   Functional question being addressed: So what? What difference does it make? (application)

8. **Subject:** The reversal of traditional distinctions of play and work
   Complement: What was play has been made into work, and what was work is now recreation.
   Functional question being addressed: What does it mean? (explanation)

Mechanical Layout of Ephesians 4:11–16

11 And he gave
    some (to be) apostles;
    and some, prophets;
    and some, evangelists;
    and some,
      pastors
      and teachers;

12 for the *perfecting* of the saints,
    unto the work of ministering,
    unto the building up of the body of Christ:

13 till we all *attain*
    unto the *unity*
      of the faith,
    and of the knowledge of the Son of God,
    unto a fullgrown man,
    unto the measure of the stature of the fulness of Christ:

14 that we may be no longer *children*,
    tossed to and fro
    and carried *about* with every wind of doctrine,
      by the sleight of men,
      in craftiness,
      after the wiles of error;

15 but speaking truth in love, may *grow up*
    in all things
    into *him*,
    who is the head,
    (even) *Christ*;

16   from whom all the body
      fitly framed
      and knit together
      through that which every joint supplieth,
      according to the working in (due) measure of
      each several part, maketh the increase of the
      body
      unto the building up of itself in love. (ASV)

Sermon-Evaluation Form

The elements of a sermon suggested in this book can be
reduced to a number of specific questions.

Organization

Introduction

Does it get attention? _____
Does it touch some need directly or indirectly? _____
Does it orient you to the subject? _____ or to the main idea?
_____ or to the first point? _____
Is it the right length? _____ Is there a specific purpose?
_____

Structure

Is the development clear? _____ Is the overall structure clear? _____

Does the sermon have a *central idea*? _____ Can you state it?_____

Are the transitions clear? _____ Do they review? _____

Is there a logical or psychological link between the points? _____

Do the main points relate back to the main idea? _____

Are the subpoints clearly related to their main points? _____

Conclusion

Does the sermon build to a climax? _____

Is there an adequate summary of ideas? _____

Are there effective closing appeals or suggestions? _____

Content

Is this subject significant? _____ Is it appropriate? _____

Is the sermon built on *solid exegesis*? _____

Does the speaker show you where he is in the text? _____

Is the analysis of the subject thorough? _____ logical? _____

Does the speaker convince you that he is right? _____

Does the content show originality? _____

Supporting Material

Is the supporting material *logically* related to its point? _____

Is it *interesting*? _____ *varied*? _____ *specific*? _____ *sufficient*? _____

Style

Does the speaker use correct grammar? _____
Is his vocabulary concrete, vivid? _____ varied? _____
Are words *used* correctly? _____
Does the choice of words add to the effectiveness of the sermon? _____

Delivery

Intellectual Directness

Does the speaker want to be heard? _____ Is he alert? _____
Do you feel he is talking with you? _____
Is he friendly? _____
Does the delivery sound like lively conversation? _____
Are words *pronounced* correctly? _____

Oral Presentation

Is the voice easy to listen to? _____ Is there clear articulation? _____

Is there vocal variety? _____ Does the *pitch* level change? _____

Is there a variety in force? _____ Does the *rate* vary enough? _____

Does the speaker use *pauses* effectively? _____

Physical Presentation

Is his entire body involved in the delivery? _____ Does he gesture? _____
Are the gestures spontaneous? _____ wide? _____ definite? _____ Are there distracting mannerisms? _____
Is the posture good? _____ Does the speaker look alert? _____

Is there good facial expression? _____

General Effectiveness

Audience Adaptation

Is the sermon adapted to your interests? _____ attitudes? _____

Is it related to your knowledge? _____ Does it meet needs? _____

Does the speaker look you in the eye? _____
Do you feel he is aware of audience response? _____

Selective Bibliography of Works Cited

Baumann, J. Daniel. *An Introduction to Contemporary Preaching*. Grand Rapids: Baker, 1972.

Beecher, Henry Ward. *Yale Lectures on Preaching*. New York: J. B. Ford, 1872.

Blackwood, Andrew W. *Expository Preaching for Today: Case Studies of Bible Passages*. Nashville: Abingdon-Cokesbury, 1953. Reprint. Grand Rapids: Baker, 1975.

Booth, John Nicholls. *The Quest for Preaching Power*. New York: Macmillan, 1943.

Brigance, William Norwood. *Speech: Its Techniques and Disciplines in a Free Society*. New York: Appleton-Century-Crofts, 1952.

Broadus, John A. *On the Preparation and Delivery of Sermons*. London: Hodder & Stoughton, 1960.

Brown, Charles R. *The Art of Preaching*. New York: Macmillan, 1922.

Bryant, Donald C., and Wallace, Karl R. *Fundamentals of Public Speaking*. New York: Appleton-Century, 1947. 3d ed. New York: Appleton-Century-Crofts, 1960.

Cox, James W. *A Guide to Biblical Preaching*. Nashville: Abingdon, 1976.

Davis, Flora. "How to Read Body Language." In *The Rhetoric of Nonverbal Communication: Readings*, edited by Haig A. Bosmajian. Glenview, Ill.: Scott, Foresman, 1971.

Davis, H. Grady. *Design for Preaching*. Philadelphia: Muhlenberg, 1958.

Dickens, Milton. *Speech: Dynamic Communication*. New York: Harcourt, Brace, 1954.

Eisenson, Jon, and Boase, Paul H. *Basic Speech*. 3d ed. New York: Macmillan, 1975.

Flesch, Rudolph. *The Art of Plain Talk*. New York: Harper, 1946.

Grasham, John A., and Gooder, Glenn G. *Improving Your Speech*. New York: Harcourt, Brace, 1960.

Gray, Giles W., and Wise, Claude M. *The Bases of Speech*. 3d ed. New York: Harper, 1959.

Hall, Edward T. *The Silent Language*. Garden City, N.Y.: Doubleday, 1959. Reprint. Greenwich, Conn.: Fawcett, 1968.

Haselden, Kyle. *The Urgency of Preaching*. New York: Harper & Row, 1963.

Hayakawa, S. I. *Language in Thought and Action*. 2d ed. New York: Harcourt, Brace & World, 1964.

Howe, Reuel L. *Partners in Preaching: Clergy and Laity in Dialogue*. New York: Seabury, 1967.

Jowett, J. H. *The Preacher: His Life and Work*. London: Hodder & Stoughton, 1912.

Macpherson, Ian. *The Art of Illustrating Sermons*. New York: Abingdon, 1964. Reprint. Grand Rapids: Baker, 1976.

Miller, Donald G. *The Way to Biblical Preaching*. New York: Abingdon, 1957.

Minnick, Wayne C. *The Art of Persuasion*. Boston: Houghton Mifflin, 1957.

Monroe, Alan H. *Principles and Types of Speech*. 3d ed. Chicago: Scott, Foresman, 1949.

Monroe, Alan H., and Ehninger, Douglas. *Principles and Types of Speech Communication*. 7th ed. Glenview, Ill.: Scott, Foresman, 1974.

Paget, Richard. *Human Speech: Some Observations, Experiments, and Conclusions as to the Nature, Origin, Purpose, and Possible Improvement of Human Speech*. New York: Harcourt, Brace, 1930.

Pelsma, John R. *Essentials of Speech*. Rev. ed. New York: Crowell, 1924.

Reid, Loren D. *Speaking Well*. Columbia, Mo.: Artcraft, 1962.

Reu, J. M. *Homiletics: A Manual of the Theory and Practice of Preaching*. Translated by Albert Steinhaeuser. Chicago: Wartburg, 1924. Reprint. Grand Rapids: Baker, 1967.

Sangster, William E. *The Craft of Sermon Construction*. Glasgow: Pickering & Inglis, new ed. 1979.

Sarrett, Alma Johnson; Sarett, Lew; and Foster, William Trufant. *Basic Principles of Speech*. 4th ed. Boston: Houghton Mifflin, 1966.

Soper, Donald O. *The Advocacy of the Gospel*. London: Hodder & Stoughton, 1961.

Stibbs, Alan M. *Expounding God's Word*. London: Inter-Varsity Press, 1960.

Sunukjian, Donald R. "Patterns for Preaching: A Rhetorical Analysis of the Sermons of Paul in Acts 13, 17, and 20." Th.D. dissertation, Dallas Theological Seminary, 1972.

Thielicke, Helmut. *Encounter with Spurgeon*. Cambridge: James Clarke, 1964.

Thompson, Wayne N. *Quantitative Research in Public Address and Communication*. New York: Random, 1967.

Thonssen, Lester, and Baird, A. Craig. *Speech Criticism: The Development of Standards for Rhetorical Appraisal*. New York: Ronald, 1948.

Tizard, Leslie J. *Preaching: The Art of Communication*. London: Allen & Unwin, 1958.

Whitesell, Faris D., ed. *Great Expository Sermons*. Westwood, N.J.: Revell, 1964.

Whitesell, Faris D., and Perry, Lloyd M. *Variety in Your Preaching*. Old Tappan, N.J.: Revell, 1954.

Williams, George G. *Creative Writing for Advanced College Classes*. Rev. ed. New York: Harper, 1954.

Wood, John. *The Preacher's Workshop: Practical Preparation for Expository Preaching*. London: Tyndale Press, 1965.

Index of Persons

227